Shades of York Street

❖

stories of friendship in the Fellowship

10 - 26. 03

FOR CALE KENNEY

WHO ALSO KNOWS

RECOVERY IN THE FELLOWSHIP.

OF FRIENDS,

THE RICHNESS POETRY

AND THE SHARING OF ONE'S STORY

CAN BRING.

LOVE,

Shades of York Street

❖

stories of friendship in the Fellowship

Nathan P.

iUniverse, Inc.
New York Lincoln Shanghai

Shades of York Street
stories of friendship in the Fellowship

iUniverse, Inc.

For information address:
iUniverse, Inc.
2021 Pine Lake Road, Suite 100
Lincoln, NE 68512
www.iuniverse.com

ISBN: 0-595-28481-7 (pbk)
ISBN: 0-595-65818-0 (cloth)

Printed in the United States of America

100 copies printed at my expense
and presented to the members
for the Fiftieth Anniversary
of the 1311 York Street Club, Inc.,
1999.
Revised and expanded
and again printed at my expense
to present to you today,
February 22, 2003

Good Luck,

Nathan P.

Contents

1

The Old Red White Elephant

You are here with me at one of the oldest Alcoholics Anonymous clubs in the world[1], 1311 York Street in Denver, a hundred year old red brick and red sandstone mansion[2] which has been a social club and meeting place for sobering drunks for more than fifty of those years. You will meet characters who are admirable and memorable, none exactly who she or he seems. There is relative happiness here, more than at any bar, but don't let that fool you—each person here has brought plenty of residual misery. One day at a time we turn misery inside-out somehow, to live real life on borrowed time. We call it a daily reprieve.

The old house is solid enough but the Club is always shaky—too little money, too few members to support the old red white elephant. Decade by decade, debacle by debacle, the Club persists, not so much by any one's heroic efforts to save it, but (for all I know) by the will of God. Whenever anyone tries to raise much money or to refurbish the innately elegant house, to upgrade wiring or to lay new carpet, it all evaporates in the egotism of those would-be heroes. So, money has been wasted or otherwise disappears, then things clunk along again much as they had been, despite all egotistic and altruistic efforts (and debt to Mister R's bank). Management frequently changes faces, but always scuttles, fudges and begs to make employment tax payments, utility bills, keep the Café open, patch the roof—all just to sustain the primary purpose, to keep the doors open for the next sick newcomer.

Bill Wilson, the first anonymous alcoholic, was here years ago[3]. His picture hangs on the wall beside Bob Smith's, that Akron proctologist who became the second founder when he got sober June 10, 1935. They are not saints, just friends whose kindness is available beyond their graves, family fathers here, so to speak. No person is in charge now, just traditions of acceptance and fellowship, barely discernible in the sometimes quiet, sometimes chaotic halls and rooms.

If pictures of all the sobering alcoholics down to the latest were here on the walls with Bill and Bob, there would be tens of thousands, many faded now. Everything changes and everything remains the same. The roots and branches of this anarchic society are kept together by a simple shared condition, a facing right into its teeth of death. For us recovering alcoholics life could not have continued in our several cold dark clouds; a need became obligatory for sunlight and for clarity, or demise would have come for each of us—should have got us each a hundred times, so it seems. We call that the turning point, the jumping off place, the bottom. Each one who wanders in would have perished alone in oblivion; only the program and the fellowship could save us for a time—to drink again and die (perhaps), or often to come to die sober, different in the last years from in the years before.

I don't feel the need to explain the history of the Twelve Step programs or the Traditions of Alcoholics Anonymous. There are simple texts available to do that for you.[4] My purpose is to describe a few real friends of mine in anonymized abbreviated form, and to ask the question how they are *together* better or stronger in their living awarenesses than they might have been. If I can touch the truth I will have shown you and me there is a way to live beyond hopelessness, beyond the narrow loneliness to which each of us is subject. Especially I wish to remind myself and you that the reliable simple beginnings of this fellowship have not been lost, and as long as we can find meaning in living one day at a time we can touch on the beginnings not only of this notable society of ex-drunks but of our own several tribes and families, to glimpse the significance of all humankind and human history.

Bill's story and Doctor Bob's are available to read[5]. Each felt alone and hopeless until they found each other. I was the same, alone and pitiful, until an old drinking buddy invited me out of my desperation into a meeting. But the story I am telling you is not about me. If what I feel is really so, I can recount the tales of several others and find the common thread which reaches to real living in community, support and reassurance for each of us.

2

An Anarchic Dis-Organization

*"**A.A., as such, ought never be organized**...[We]
could do no more than make suggestions...[A]lcoholics
can't be dictated to...Unless each A.A. member follows
to the best of [her or] his ability our suggested Twelve
Steps to recovery, [she or] he almost certainly signs [her
or] his own death warrant. [Her or h]is drunkenness
and dissolution are not penalties inflicted by people in
authority; they result from [her or] his personal disobedi-
ence to spiritual principles...Great suffering and great
love are A.A.'s disciplinarians...It is the difference
between the spirit of vested authority and the spirit of
service...A.A. has to function, but at the same time it
must avoid those dangers of great wealth, prestige, and
entrenched power which necessarily tempt other societ-
ies."*

—Bill Wilson (on the Ninth Tradition)
<u>Twelve Steps and Twelve Traditions</u> (1952)

"For us, to drink is to die."

It seems one thing our members have in common is a great
difficulty following instructions. We have too many conceits
of righteousness or altruism to do as someone else tells us.

These are merely blatant manifestations of ego, obvious enough to any objective observer but invisible to each of its victims (or perpetrators). Each of us decides what's best for everyone else, and tries to make them do it by intimidation, flattery, railroading or stealth. We have known this from the time we started in 1935.

We had to find a different way to operate and relate to each other; somehow, sometimes, we have succeeded. We use some terms which initially may sound strange to describe a new different basis for our decisions and actions. We get used to these terms, find them familiar to us soon: "group conscience," "God's will," "higher power" and such.

It boils down to a simple shift in the meaning of self and the meaning of an other. I am no longer seeking to fulfill my own goals, using others as objects toward my own ends. I seek to be of service to my higher power and to my fellow human beings. That's the simple truth, and although I will never do it perfectly I make efforts at it and progress toward it every day.

One of the most potent practical tools toward this change from a self-centered existence to a spiritually centered life is the fearless and thorough moral inventory through which I have assessed the destructiveness of my self-centeredness. Perhaps some others can get along behaving conventionally, but not us drunks. We have worn out anger and selfishness long since, and will certainly die (and likely destroy others in the process) if we again wallow in self-will.

All of this is detailed in our unmystical practical published text, the Big Book, <u>Alcoholics Anonymous</u>. It has been validated anew millions of times with remarkable consistency. There are other approaches to recovery from alcoholism (and similar human ailings such as addiction and compulsive eating) but they either are based on a radical revision of attitudes and behaviors toward self and others, or they run the risk of rekindling "self-will run riot" from which we already suffer. None of us admits these egotistic faults willingly, so we must be "beaten into a state of reasonableness" by our disease before we can begin to recover.

We can't undo the past, but we can effectively avoid repeating it. Each of us knows if *we* can get sober anyone can. Getting sober and staying sober are essential for us, demand our lifelong communal energy and effort. We have to do more than merely to stay dry, but we don't know exactly how. Now I will stop lecturing or preaching (uninstructive always) to tell you true stories (always enlightening), but just for another moment bear with me so I can sketch what seems an unmapped territory beyond mere sobriety.

Human culture and human history seem mostly self-centered. Those times and places which seem to us less individualistic and less materialistic than our own seem little different from each other in this regard, because they have substituted the investment of ego into powerful other individuals or institutions (the State, the Church, the Race, the Cause). We human beings seem almost always to act as if we are right and anyone who differs must be wrong. We are judgmental at the core, pretend sometimes to join others, but when it comes right down to it we act as if the only relationships we have are competitions, not partnerships.

Maybe we alcoholics constitute good examples of human faults, and perhaps our recovery can be exemplary of potential remedies thereof. We have come together in our desire to stop drinking. We don't care so much about why we drink as how not to, one day at a time. Perhaps we drank because we suffered individually the faults of all humans as an aggregate. Perhaps we manifested selfishness and competition more severely than most, or perhaps we were more sensitive to the discomfort of universal alienation and hostility almost always inherent in human society. Whatever the causes, our solution is in human community (the unique pioneering effort of our anarchic dis-organization).

We subscribe to no theology, though we tend to come (kicking and screaming mostly) to seeking relation to a higher power. It is no god, though we tend to call it God. Some of us call it Skippy or Charlie. We don't have to call it anything, for we do not together see it or name it, but live in relation to it. We call our attitude spiritual rather than religious. If we did not look to an Other as the source of truth we would be back in self immediately, drunk again. For us it would be dishonesty, for we already proved Self is not the center of the universe. (Recall Warty Bliggins the Toad, Don Marquis' character reported by humble Archy the Cockroach; or Toad of Toad Hall, Kenneth Grahame's classic alcoholic manic reflection of his untamable inner self, who repeatedly had to be rescued by his more humble and more responsible friends Ratty, Mole and Badger[6].)

Any approach to recovery that looks to some standard higher than the individual self could work as ours does, I suppose. We find it safer for us not to specify that standard, to try to relate to it without institutionalizing it. Any approach to recovery which relies on obedience to authority, however, we doubt could work with the likes of us. Any approach to authority which seeks to clean up the self, to reestablish the self as the authority, scares us witless; each of us struggles to step clear of that quagmire every day.

We have learned we can't do it alone. We must somehow do it together; that is our First Tradition. If all human culture and human history have not yet begun to solve the problems of selfishness, alienation and hostility in human life, how can we sickos easily do it? We cannot easily do it, but we can avoid the errors of the past, seek new means no matter how strange they may sound ("group conscience," "higher power," even "*God*'s will").

3

My Own First Sponsors

The word 'sponsor' does not occur in the first couple hundred pages of the Big Book (the basic old part, essentially unchanged from 1939). I watch some people in the program agonizing over sponsors, as if their sobriety depended on some other person (which the Big Book definitely denies). Ebby T. 'sponsored' Bill Wilson, the old drinking buddy who came to Bill sober one day and convinced him there was a way out even for a hopeless drunk like Bill. Bill sponsored Ebby, tried to help him get sober for the remaining years of Ebby's life, but Ebby died drunk. We share the disease, and we share the solution.

I have come to consider we all sponsor each other. When people talk about 'firing' a sponsor and getting a new one, it puzzles me. A sponsor is someone whose suggestions I try to follow carefully only because "my own best thinking got me where I am." No one helps any of us stay sober more effectively than the 'wet' newcomer, and no one helps us firm up the life-giving work of the program more arduously than the newcomer we help through the Steps. We say the most important person in any meeting is the newcomer, and we act that way, cheering and welcoming her or him. Seeing a newcomer in a meeting brings to the surface the newcomer in me; helping that person by being available and open is my best way of comforting the newcomer in me who was desperately afraid he was alone forever.

Each of the persons in these anecdotes has really been my sponsor; I have thousands of them, millions. I am very wealthy in sponsors whose stories are like mine. My story is no different from any other drunk's; the details always sound different, but the plot is always the same. Details and differences aren't very important; it is the shared story of every alcoholic which lets us help each other to become sober and to recover our humanity.

We don't know or understand our stories when we first come in; we have to figure them out gradually. ("More will be revealed.") I drank as fast and hard as I could from age six to age forty-three, the booze stopped working and I was so suicidal I couldn't drink, so when an old drinking buddy three years sober asked me if I wanted to come to a meeting I said yes and everything began to change.

My strong values, will and determination had no effect whatsoever. It was not a question of my waning strengths or virtues, but of my unacknowledged character defects. It took time to begin to acknowledge them without beating myself up over them (since I could no longer afford to deny them). It helped a lot to be with persons who shared them, accepted them and did not blame me for my faults. ("Did your chicken die, too?")

I wasn't in very good condition for human contact when I first came into A.A. I immediately and for the first time in my life felt I was not alone, but I couldn't really talk with anyone else; what they said made no sense to me, and what I said made no sense at all. It wasn't a matter of making sense, but just being there, together.

I heard them say to get a sponsor to help me do the work. I wanted to do what they said, but I was used to helping other people, not the other way around. I wanted my sober friend to sponsor me, but he declined saying we were too close, too much like brothers. (Two years later I declined to sponsor my own brother, for the same reasons; but by then I had begun to accept and understand things I could not easily explain.) I looked for someone who could help me, but most of them looked terribly faulty and needy themselves (to my picky perfectionistic eye). The ones who looked okay seemed either haughty and full of themselves or blindly obedient to the incomprehensible text of the Big Book.

I tried to work with a very nice fellow, but he was in the midst of prolonged unemployment and painful divorce, so I saw him as more needy than I. I omitted noting my own crises of prolonged unemployment, impending divorce, civil charges, criminal charges, bankruptcy, failing health, foreclosure on the house, repossession of the car, alienation from my children, prolonged and profound depression, and all the more important problems I haven't listed. I also omitted to note that, unlike me, he was sober (the only thing I had real need for—"If you want what we have…" refers to sobriety, not all the other stuff.)

I couldn't work, I couldn't make sense, I couldn't relate to another human being. All I could do was to dream.

Bill Wilson (who had died sixteen years earlier) came to me in my dreams frequently and candidly. He was tall and grey and kind. He moved gingerly so that I had to hustle to try to keep up with him. He spoke directly, simply and tersely. He spoke to *me*.

> "Nathan, Bob and I are going to take care of you until you get well enough to talk to another living person. Just go to meetings, read the Big Book and pay attention to your dreams."

> "Bill, I really appreciate the attention, and I admit I really need it; but you keep saying you and Doctor Bob are going to take care of me, and I never see Bob."

> "Oh, don't worry about that. I'm sorta the mouthpiece of this organization. Bob's kinda quiet, but he's here with us. You don't need to see him to be with him. Now, what have you learned about your drinking?"

> "It's just like yours, hopeless."

> "Keep dreaming; you're making progress."

The most vivid of these several dreams stays with me. Like dreams are usually, it seemed quite real to the dreamer then, although its "facts" didn't fit conventional reality. The impact and the meaning were clear to me at the time, have grown one day at a time, as I have.

All appearances in a dream are, in fact the dreamer. Sigmund Freud and I are convinced of that. My real daughter has protested that I shouldn't call her an alcoholic until she has had her first drink. She considers all infants suck the foam from the bottom of beer bottles as she did (if their sloppy drunk fathers line them up there on the porch on a lovely summer day). "But not so hard they pull the labels off from the inside," I rejoin.

> I was in a small neat brick house, another place, another time (I could clearly feel the difference from the present). It was like my grandparents' house, but not exactly like the one I could remember; maybe it was the one in which I had lived with them during my infancy, during the Second World War.

> People were there, friendly and familiar, but I didn't see them. I was looking for my infant daughter (who at that "real" time I was dreaming was no longer an infant at all). I asked everyone if they had seen her, where she had gone.

> It was indeed the Nineteen-forties. As I ran up and down the neighborhood looking for my baby I sensed the bright summer air, the buildings, cars and dress of that time I knew so well, before my memory perhaps, but what I had learned in detail from the faces and voices of the big people when I had been an infant.

I knew Bill Wilson was coming through that town, my home town. He was on his way to California. He was leaving on the train at exactly eleven twenty, and it was now beyond the eleventh hour. I had to find my daughter, to have her meet him before it was too late.

I tried to stay calm, efficient, but I didn't have much time. I rushed about the house and neighborhood looking and asking for my daughter. Time rushed away from me like water, I couldn't hold it back. I couldn't hold time (couldn't hold my water).

(The morning she was born in fact, I was surprised. She was weeks early. The water broke. We calmly and efficiently went to the obstetrician's office. He assured us it would be hours, her mother's cervix just beginning to dilate. He would meet us at the hospital later, when labor had progressed. At the labor deck I changed into a surgical scrub suit, as I was instructed, not to be a doctor but a father. I turned to see she was crowning, her head protruding from her mother's vulva. I called the nurse, began to push the bed (on casters) toward the delivery room holding her in with the palm of my hand so she wouldn't pop out and bounce on the floor. The intern—a competent and calm colleague to me many years since—had never delivered a baby; I had done it hundreds of times, but this time I was the father, not the doctor. I couldn't let myself help her, but my daughter did help her, coming out small and easy, natural, gay and enthusiastic. The obstetrician showed up later. Nothing was quite the way he or I had prescribed. Real life doesn't seem to go by textbooks or the expectations of male doctors.)

I rushed about the neighborhood as calmly and as efficiently as I could, looking for my baby girl; but time rushed on and I became more frantic, redisciplined myself, slowed down purposely in my haste, lowered my voice. The train would leave on time; it always did those days, or in my dreams. I didn't stop to think exactly why I had to have my baby meet Bill Wilson, but it was everything to me in that dream.

I finally found her crawling about and playing in the dirt under the front porch of that little brick house. I was relieved. I was afraid the time was too short, but I knew not to frighten or alarm her by grabbing her up abruptly. I knelt down with her under the porch, reached out to her, took her in my arms, cooed to her we would go together to have a treat, something fun, someone new to meet. I stood carefully from under the porch (roomy to that baby but cramped for me), calmly considered whether to take the car or walk the few blocks, so I put her securely under my arm like a football—and ran like hell straight across the town, over fences, down across the railroad tracks, up the street huffing, sweating, panting, rushing to the little train station where the big engine stood even now belching clouds of steam, chugging, splitting the still summer air with its siren announcing immediate departure.

I ran even faster than full speed, the sinking feeling of failure pressing the last bit of breath out of my chest, to the clanking wooden platform. To my relief I saw a group of people slowly, calmly climbing onto the train. Mister Wilson stood tall in the middle, airy and bright as the summer day in his blue seersucker suit, his light Panama. He was near the door to the train car, but casually turned as I called him, not rushed, not irritated. He smiled, his brow inquiring how he might help.

I held my smiling baby up to him, and he returned her smile. No word was said. They had met, and I was thankful, truly calm at last. She would not remember, as she grew, but I would remind her. She had met Bill Wilson one lovely summer day.

4

Bridging the Gap

I have come to see the game of bridge as an exemplary model for recovery: You must take the hand that's dealt you. You must assess its strengths and weaknesses. You must communicate effectively with your partner. You must take action by the rules of the game. And the outcome does not at all depend on your own will or wishes, excuses or protests.

A.A. meetings at the York Street club take place on the second and third floors, but a relatively constant small meeting occurs most any afternoon at the front table in the first floor lounge—the bridge game. We sometimes call this the First Floor Prayer Meeting.

Several other members of the Club look on the bridge players with disdain. They see them playing cards, so they imagine they never see them upstairs at meetings. Some bridge players avoid A.A. meetings, not most. The cynics can't perceive them individually in meetings, having seen them as a group downstairs.

What they don't realize is that now a majority of the Board of the Club are bridge players, and we're aiming to have all seven seats. It's not to take control, of course, but to have short meetings. If an eighth bridge player shuffles the cards while the other seven are in the Board meeting upstairs once a month, the Club's business can be transacted quickly, and two tables of bridge can fill the rest of the evening.

What is important is that most bridge players stay sober. They have a fellowship which encourages sobriety, even though the idiom of their conversation comes more from the classic text, the bridge player's Big Book (Five Weeks to Winning Bridge by Alfred Sheinwold). Aspiring bridge players are told to read the first three chapters of the book, then to come back and talk about it. Like aspiring recoverers they may not return soon or ever, but if they do they become part of something ongoing, a tradition which remembers specific hands and bridge players long gone.

At York Street one can stay sober not only playing bridge but playing pinochle. Pinochle is a very different game, manifests differently the realities of life and sobriety. To a bridge player the pinochle hand looks very rich (twenty cards instead of thirteen, all high cards); which strikes me as parallel to the seeming difference between the newcomer to A.A. who has just crawled out from under a bridge and the one who still has a watch (the "high bottom" or "silk sheet" drunk). But you can lose at pinochle, too.

Pinochle shares the sobering virtues of most games, that you must accept and follow arbitrary rules (ordinarily a difficult task for an alcoholic). Card games tend to force even the angry distracted newcomer into a semblance of social decorum. Even though the stakes are nominal, cheating is as unthinkable and intolerable as disruptiveness in an A.A. meeting. (Cheating finally closed the poker game in the York Street basement, which had been lucrative for the Club but more lucrative for the con-artists.) Now we play for the fellowship, not to grab the money.

It is said most pinochle players learned the game in the army or in jail, but that is not what makes it a violent game. The violence of pinochle is always aimed at one's partner, very simply because partners don't rotate as they do in bridge. In the bridge rotation used at York Street (called the Chicago variation) you can be frustrated by your partner's poor bidding or play, but you know he will be your opponent twice as often as he will be your partner, so you tolerate him in anticipation of pocketing his money at the end of the session. In pinochle, to have an erratic or stubbornly egotistic partner is disaster.

From time to time I see groups of younger persons playing Spades. They are always animated and social. Hearts could be the same, but I never see it played at York Street.

Cribbage is a two- or three-person game which can be played silently. It allows smooth flow of the game at the same time as smooth flow of conversation, so real dialogue about recovery can take place along with the game. Many times Big George and I have discussed my problems of living while he has beaten me at cribbage, and sometimes we have helped a newcomer while we played the game, explaining we are listening carefully to his story all along.

Chess may be the most violent game played at the Club. Although it is always played in silence, it is competition pure and simple, an uncompromising effort to vanquish the other. The usual chess players are rough types, manual laborers and cynical loners. They can stay sober too.

There are a few old video games and a pinball machine in the room between the office and the vestibule itself (known as D.P.R.[7]). I call that game room Seth's Office because my brother Seth sobered up playing the pinball machine, or rather beating on it and cursing at it. Rich C. played Ms. Pacman for two years, got his name on all the first ten winners' lines, then returned to his office downtown to work sober. Those machines provoke or suffer more violence even than chess because they allow a ragged newcomer to take out his frustrations on a broken old machine.

What is rarely acknowledged consciously by any of us is that the person noisily alone in the little game machine room really acts as if he is struggling with the *entire universe*—switches, lights and innards he cannot himself control. When the maddened newcomer has exhausted himself or mastered the machine he may graduate to a more humble smaller real world, maybe even sit down in D.P.R. to talk recovery with other real persons.

The point of reviewing games in recovery is simple: that we learn to follow rules. Bridge continues daily, perhaps because it involves four or five or more persons in a formalized set of behaviors limited by a deck of fifty-two cards. Pinochle has unchanging partners (the way we play it), more cards, so more mindless luck. Cribbage uses less persons, less cards, but is even more mindless, so we can talk while playing. Chess is very personal but directly competitive. Machines leave a person alone, but facing the limitations inherent in the program or structure of a machine. Whatever way you cut it, games give us a chance calmly to compete within the rules instead of uncomfortably and impossibly to straddle the limitless oblivion of drunkenness struggling in mortal combat with every thing and every one.

5

Even Cowboys Get the Booze

He taught me ineducability: I too wanted to be a cowboy when I was a little boy—two guns, single minded. I couldn't be told anything by anyone; and if they tried to teach me I'd blow them away. As I think about my old cowboy friend I begin to see what we can suffer when we can't live life on life's terms, when we are always too ready to impose our own terms on life. Even the best of us are deeply stubborn, individualistic hero gun-slingers. We can die sober, but on the way there may be a lot of heartaches (and heart attacks).

Sophisticated cowboy, tall, dark handsome and glib, he had drunk all he could stand to drink. Before he fell into recovery, finally to die a quarter of a century sober, he had slipped from a fast-talking country and western singer, super-salesman, entrepreneur executive to a sad bowed old man, a has-been. Alcohol had brought him to his knees or lower long before character flaws and age could do him in.

If there is anything good about hitting bottom it is never having to go that low again. This fellow had a second life coming in sobriety, but until he got sober he couldn't see it because it wasn't there.

Two families gone, careers in railroading and in sales down the drain, but Texas and New Mexico remained unchanged, raucous territory rapidly booming where everybody drawled, everybody hustled, everybody drank whiskey. Only this cowboy seemed to have become depleted, drained. Booze had licked him, and he wanted to find a way to fight back.

But he couldn't fight. He was drunk out and he was fought out. It was all over, again. This time it seemed there was no taking a deep breath, splashing cold water on his face, hitching up his jeans and going back into the fray. This time there was no bravado; the booze had decked him for the last time.

Life may not always have been easy, but always exciting. Somehow he had scraped through the tough world of the Great Depression like it was a circus, and he was at once the happy awe-struck kid and at the same time the star of the show, magically and fantastically performing while he watched himself in the mirror; and the world around him cooperated, applauded, loved him. There was no nagging fear it would collapse or he would fall from the high-wire, for he believed in himself as completely as the world around him did. He was his own hero.

His mom was loving and provident, but tough as leather, the kind of rigid moralist one learns to seduce into collusion with one's pranks. His dad seemed simply mean, "an alcoholic who doesn't drink," the kind of authoritarian one learns to evade, someday finally to confront toe to toe. His brothers were his partners and his protégés, sometimes his dupes. He never understood exactly what turned him and them into raging alcoholics, finally beaten.

But youth was a ball in that topsy-turvy world. He skated through military school without being busted. Through family and friends he got a job on the railroad as a lowly laborer, and soon was in charge of the gang, the kind of young hot-shot whose lack of years the bosses wanted hidden lest his authority as a foreman be disdained.

It could have made a secure career, rapidly rolling upward on the railroad, but what promise does investment in reality hold compared to night life's immediate payoffs? Playing the guitar and singing with his brother in country and western dance bands was much more glamorous, so he went for it, went for the smoke and noise and intoxication and girls. It was like the choice between school and the circus. No contest.

He didn't have time to realize that dance clubs and honky-tonks might have their depressing aspects. He skipped like a stone over the surface, not yet sinking to the depths, bouncing high one more time, and another, and the next.

The War had come, brought soldiers and sailors into the juke joints, made action lively. He was too young to enlist when it started, but was conscripted before it was over. That was not so bad; he was always able to be energetic and cheerful in what seemed to others adverse circumstances.

The Quartermaster Corps at the end of the war in Italy gave him the opportunity to be a wheeler-dealer in all kinds of stuff. When he was in boot camp booze was cheap in the enlisted man's club, but now as a lieutenant he was in charge of warehouses full of the stuff, for free. He controlled building supplies, food, clothing, everything anyone could want, and the fleets of vehicles to move them anywhere in Europe.

He rapidly went up in rank, no problem with drinking because his drinking buddies were his superiors in rank, generals who would never bust him for disappearing for a weekend with a truck full of Italian girls, a case of booze and a guitar.

When the war was over he went back out west, to Houston where everything was booming. He played and sang just like he was still in Italy. Night club connections, his energy and ebullience, got him a day job in medical sales, specifically surgical supplies, especially orthopedic.

High technology was the name of the game, so the manufacturer's representative had to instruct the surgeon how to use new hip prostheses and such. It seemed natural enough for this cowboy to scrub into surgery, pretty much take over the operation. What need was there for medical training when you had blarney and panache?

It went on for a long while, wheeling and dealing in the big new medical institutions, hob-nobbing on a first-name basis with the elite of the medical profession, entertaining on a grand scale in tailored western-cut suits, driving Cadillacs, having women chasing you, and whiskey.

Respectable job and second family, house in the suburbs, opportunity for stability in the long term didn't change his underlying attitude a bit; he was still a brash bronc-rider whooping, hooting and hollering through little old Texas. The ride would never stop.

The last thing we alcoholics give up is the job. Any job seems tough if you don't know how to do it, but give us one day to learn the ropes and we can do it blind-folded, or hung over. We cruise through life like tornadoes, too strong and fast for anyone to call our bluff…until that inevitable day, we slip once or stumble on our own clumsy feet, step on other people's feet.

It doesn't matter exactly how it happened; it was in the cards all along, though he could never see it himself. All the warnings and sincere exhortations for moderation went unheeded, never registered in his brilliant scintillating brain. He didn't kill a patient in the operating room, although he might have. He didn't run over a school bus full of nuns in his Cadillac convertible, although that had always been a risk. He didn't shoot some bad guy in a blackout, perhaps only because he didn't carry a gun.

Most likely he just didn't take care of his sales accounts, started being late instead of early, missed appointments, made lame excuses. He slipped over the line subtly, the next drink more important than the next phone call, nursing the hangover taking priority over riding herd on the doctors for the sake of the corporation.

He had had a clue before, a little hint, but he had ignored it as thoroughly as possible. (Real rodeo cowboys have learned to ignore broken bones, so hot-shot medical reps certainly can ignore hangovers and blackouts.) He had been to an A.A. meeting some time in the confusion of his previous divorces, but he hadn't let it slow him down. Now that the job was gone, however, so went the Cadillac, the bravado, the night life.

Despite fantasies of repairing the damage, the crushing reality hit him like a bullet in the chest: the job was gone, and with it all hope. Marriage, family, all the rest mattered, but were not essential to his existence. Loss of his job meant his personal freedom to run wild had run out. The booze had stopped working. It no longer could help him resurrect his fantasies. All he knew was that he had been bucked off his high horse and couldn't get back on again (and this time he didn't really want to).

A telephone call to the intergroup office in Houston got him a ride to a meeting easily enough. Despite his restless, irritable and discontented state he had nothing better to do than to take a ride in the back seat for once. It was the beginning of a real ride, a wild ride, a long ride, an unpredictable and exciting ride. It was the beginning of nearly thirty years of sobriety, but that night he couldn't know it yet. It was his thirty-ninth birthday. Whoopee! A different sort of party, indeed.

Easy does it, sure, but it was hard to keep him from picking up speed once he got to rolling. Within a short couple years of sobriety he started a halfway house for alcoholic jailbirds, a project never before tried. His experiences sounded to me a lot like Bill Wilson's and Doctor Bob's thirty-five years earlier. It was slow going, frustrating trying to get a project started on nothing but a shoe string and a ten gallon hat full of enthusiasm. The only bitter memory of all of it was that when he had two residents the first Christmas they couldn't sing carols because a third had absconded with his only guitar (hocked it for a drink).

The halfway house didn't make him rich or famous, but got the attention of some of the politically influential who were interested in the treatment of alcoholism. He got a grant from the National Institute on Alcoholism to move to Denver to run a fourteen state program on alcohol rehabilitation coordinated with OEO projects, part of the War on Poverty. But Nixon came into office and froze the funds, so that was nixed.

Colorado politicians were interested in promoting a bill to decriminalize alcoholism (including former liberals like Dick Lamm). The Alcohol and Drug Abuse Division of the Colorado State Health Department hired him as a sort of lobbyist to promote the bill to the legislature. When the measure passed, the State kept him on to set up all the alcohol-related treatment programs. He wrote and lobbied for the Colorado regulations, which became the model for most of the other states.

So, less than five years sober, this cowboy had formulated much of the national approach to the treatment of alcoholism as a disease, not a crime. His approach was always pragmatic, keeping as a priority the welfare of the real individual alcoholic, eschewing bureaucracy. (He told his secretary to summarize only the "musts" from the legislature, all of which would be done to the letter, and to consider anything not mandatory as flexible, discretionary.)

He and all his friends in A.A. and alcohol treatment knew his energetic efforts were simply meant to help the suffering alcoholic. If he seemed opinionated or stubborn it was only to help those who were down. His colleagues in government watched him use the criterion of the welfare of the real individual alcoholic or addict. Yet he could not easily understand relapse as part of the disease; having himself been relieved of the compulsion to drink, he couldn't countenance anyone giving in to it again.

He promoted recovering alcoholics as counselors to be trained and qualified in state licensed facilities, but he always regretted the elaborate training and certification requirements which were subsequently added, the massive bureaucracy with which treatment facilities were subsequently burdened. He had inadvertently "created" the industry of for-profit alcohol and addiction treatment, the new "profes-sion" of certified alcohol counselors.

He was recognized by those who cared about alcoholism as a pioneer. Despite having contributed much to the creation of the industry and the profession, later he could not get a job in either of them. He tried starting up treatment centers with other recovering professionals, but none of them worked out well for long.

Even though he had his long moment in the sun, some years of prominence and success pioneering for effective humane alcoholism treatment, he ended his days out to pasture, champing at the bit, still an idiosyncratic loner, still a fire-brand. As modest circumstances took away the big powerful automobiles he drove the little clunkers all the harder and faster, delivering pizzas instead of lobbying the legislatures.

The wife he had thirteenth-stepped back in Houston was too strong not to become frustrated in his shadow. She also was sober twenty-five years, worked in institutions treating alco-holics. Their lives were similar and should have fit, but he had a tendency to try to dominate, and as he got older and weaker after his sixth heart attack he couldn't get away with that. She had her own ideas and aspirations, so after decades of being a nurse she started study for the priesthood, and separated from him. She took him back just before the end, for no doubt she loved the brash cowboy.

Like all of us he died imperfect, still restless, irritable and dis-contented, but sober and not alone. No, he was not alone. At

his funeral her new church was packed, not even any standing room, as she bravely conducted services for hundreds of
his friends and colleagues. At the front of the podium were
his ashes serenely resting in a cowboy boot.

6

Big George

This morning George faces another life and death crisis, another surgery.[8] When a decade ago I first saw him at the York Street Club he had been an installation on the first floor for some years already. I can bring the image vividly to my eye of a hulk of a man nodding rhythmically asleep in a straight chair at the front table of the lounge, his canes propped next to him against the window sill. He sits waiting for three other bridge players or one other cribbage player, reads military and spy novels, naps upright.

I couldn't help seeing that his bulk, inertia imposed by back pain, his swollen feet and his easy somnolence were likely signs of 'Ondine's curse'—sleep apnea. He told me he could not rest at night, especially because of his back pain (and I imagined he awakened anoxic, aware of the pain in his back but awake because his soft palate had repeatedly obstructed his airway like a flappy one-way valve). I shuddered to think of trying to sleep myself, were I to spend a night in the same room with his resonant snore.

George had come to York Street nearly twenty-three years ago to get a drink. He knew an A.A. club was a good place to borrow a couple of bucks, that people in A.A. would under-stand what it means to need a drink. It was winter, and he had been living under a viaduct. He knew he was better than the bums under the bridge or the fools in the A.A. club, just temporarily down on his luck. Things were not going so well, but he didn't give that much thought, just went from moment to moment, town to town in his big body driven by its big ego.

He didn't get the handout he wanted. The bitch behind the desk cheerily offered to let him shovel the walk for a sand-wich and a cup of coffee. He didn't know why he said okay and took the shovel in hand, since he knew he didn't think her offer was worth a...the trouble.

A fellow strode out of the building and up to George.

"Let's go get a drink."

"One drink won't do it."

"Let's go get drunk."

"You don't have enough money to get me drunk."

"I have enough to get us both drunk," as he pulled a wad of bills from his pocket.

"Naw, I told that lady I'd shovel the walk. Go on with-out me."

George doesn't know to this day what made him do that. He knew even then it wasn't in his repertory to decline a drink. He doesn't know why he said he'd shovel the walk when he meant to tell her off for offering a cheese sandwich and a cup of coffee when he needed a drink.

George doesn't know to this day what made him hang around York Street, except an almost unconscious curiosity overshadowed by doubt, that if these people really had something... He remembers he was very big and very angry, and he resented every smile and platitude. Somehow Wally W. picked him up early, Wally the con man who had spent the previous few years sobering up in San Francisco, conning the price of a drink from the people in A.A. there, sometimes leaving the meeting early to steal the battery from a car in the parking lot, often staying in the meeting long enough to take some money out of the basket as it came around to him. But Wally hadn't had a drink in a long while. Wally had enough ego to take on a rough newcomer like George, relished instructing such a big lost angry boy in immediate practicalities.

> "You can be as mad as you want, but you can't hit anyone first. If they hit you first, though, you can hit them back. Got it?"

> "Got it."

So George stood angrily blocking the hallway, waiting for someone to brush against him. All he wanted to do was to slug someone.

> "You can't just stand around here bumming cigarettes, waiting for someone to buy you a sandwich. Go get a job."

George got a job.

"I got a job, but I hate it."

"Quit."

"But you told me to get a job."

"I didn't tell you to keep it."

George quit his job. The next day Wally saw him standing around at the Club.

"Why aren't you at work?"

"You told me to quit my job."

"I didn't tell you not to get another."

George had fifty-four jobs his first year sober. The I.R.S. didn't want to believe him, but he had all the W-2's in chronologic order.

George hated God. No one was going to tell George what to do. Wally told George God would take care of him. George didn't believe it. For thirty-three years only George could take care of George, but not quite well enough. His dad had taught him how to fight in bars, had told him how his clan were so belligerent they frightened the Romans away from Ireland in 500 BC. Since his clan successfully had been drinking and fighting since before the Roman Church came to Ireland with Saint Patrick, what use did George have for the Church?

George didn't trust God. Not only did he have to take care of himself, but no one else would wish to do it, especially God. Little though he understood it, these people at York Street seemed calm and happy, and they said they were sober. If there was even a little chance it were true, or at least that it was a good scam…

George's lack of understanding didn't come from lack of intelligence. He had first done hard time at fourteen, the result of hard life in many rough cities. At eighteen he went to college from the prison, part of an experimental program to rehabilitate some of the misdirected geniuses of tender years then the wards of the State of California. College let George out of his cell and into the bars where students drank. He had to return from the dormitory to the prison for weekends, so he told the other students he was going home (as if he had one). The guards checked the curfew time exactly, but not George's breath.

Out in the world after his release he had several successful businesses, at which he failed. He blamed his employees rather than his drunkenness. As legitimate businesses disintegrated, it was not difficult for George (because of his intimidating size) to get odd jobs in another sort of enterprise, collecting debts for the mob.

His defiance of authority didn't suit to be an organization man, and his obedience to instructions was compromised by the discontinuity of blackouts. Once he awakened in a motel room—that didn't surprise him. He looked for a drink, but all the bottles were empty—that didn't surprise him, but concerned him. He reached for the phone to call for a bottle or to find out which way the bar was. He noticed on the telephone the area code wasn't familiar. He looked it up. He was a thousand miles off course. That surprised him. He checked to see if he had enough money in his pockets for a bottle—none. He checked around the room for loose change, finally opened the window shade from which there fell a wad of eighteen thousand dollars. With some concern he thought to check his gun—one bullet fired. At what? To this day he doesn't know.

The mysterious money disappeared as easily as it always does, especially running from the mob *and* the cops. A few months and a few towns later George found himself under a bridge in Denver. At least, he reassured himself, he was not one of those uneducated bums under the bridge. No, he thought…he was one of the educated ones. So he came to York Street to scrape up enough money for a drink.

George did not trust God, but he did trust Wally (which seems to me the greater leap of faith). He decided he needed an automobile to get to work. Wally and all the others kept telling George to ask God for what he needed. George had not the slightest inclination to try that, so he did. He asked God to get him a car, to save him from a bus ride an hour and a half each way. He walked into the Club mumbling his prayer, "God, if you want me to have a car, get me a car, dammit." Collins C. immediately said to him, "George, I know a lady who has a car for sale, if you want one, a 1960

Corvair for thirty-five dollars." George had forty dollars in his pocket, which convinced him for the moment God's will was that he have the car and still not be flat broke.

"I've come to see about your car."

"Oh, yes. It's a fine automobile. I think you'll like it. I got a new one, but I sure hate giving that one up. The Bel Air is a nice model, and a hundred and thirty-five dollars is pretty cheap, I think."

"Bel Air? But Collins said a Corvair, for thirty-five."

"Oh, that. Yes, it's out there too, but my son promised it to a friend of his."

"Well, since I came all the way out here could I look at it?"

"Sure, but I think you'll like the Bel Air better."

"Ma'am, I'm a recovering alcoholic. I don't have much money, but I need to get back and forth to work. I need to get the cheapest car I can find."

George looked at the Corvair; it was rusted and rotted, but it started. He looked at the Bel Air; it was the most beautiful machine he had ever laid eyes on.

"I'll take the Corvair."

"But I can't sell it to you. My son promised it to his friend for twenty-five dollars."

"I'll pay him thirty."

"A promise is a promise."

George had the distinct righteous impulse to throw the kid through the wall for opposing God's will. But, he had to pause when agitated (as he had been instructed), then he'd bash the kid.

"Well, I can't afford any Bel Air. Thanks anyhow."

"Wait. You like that Bel Air, don't you? I know it would get you to work better than the Corvair. Try it. It's a good car. I drove it for years myself. I want it to have a good home."

George drove the Bel Air to work. He loved it. The engine worked, the cigarette lighter worked, the clock worked, even the spotlight worked. He took it back to the woman.

"I'm working right now, but I don't know how I could get a hundred thirty-five dollars. I'm sure it's worth it, but that's more than I can get."

"You seem like a sincere young man. How about twenty-five now and twenty-five a month? Could you do that?"

"Why would you do that for me?"

"I'm not an alcoholic, George, but I believe in the same God you do. You'd be doing me a favor. I don't need the money today as much as I may need it later, and that car has been good to me. I want to see that car have good care and good use."

She signed the title over to him, took his twenty-five dollars. George took the car. He made the next payment, but then he broke his hand at work, so there went the income. He knew he should tell the lady, but couldn't get himself to communicate with her. His hand healed finally, and he got another job, but soon was fired. There was no way he could pay her what he owed her. He just hoped none of those self-righteous types at the Club would ask him why he was driving a car he hadn't paid for.

Those W-2's paid off. George got a refund from the IRS for two hundred fifty-two dollars. Driving down the street in his 1959 Bel Air, he began to dream of what he could do with so much money. He imagined he could go to Miami where no one knew him, start over again. Then he thought of San Francisco where he knew a lot of people, where he could go to meetings, get on his feet. He was thinking what a great party he could have with that money in Cheyenne right up the highway, away from those glum sober types at the Club, just turn onto I-25, cruise north for an hour—when he pulled up into the lady's driveway. Puzzled, since he had had no intention of driving to her house, he knocked on the door.

"I knew you'd come today."

"Huh?"

"My son got a free trip to Europe with the school band. All I have to do is pay the tax on his ticket, eighty-five dollars. I wondered where I would get it, then I knew you'd come today."

So, George came to believe, not just for that moment but over and over again. Every time he thought he knew God's will he found anew that God, indeed, was taking care of him, but not the way George's imagination had concocted it. "The bitch about trusting God is trusting God," George often says.

George learned over and over to trust God. He studied hard, became an ordained minister, visions of fame and fortune for himself, faith healing on the television, another Billy Graham. But that was ego, so he kept driving a cab, trusting God often, slipping occasionally into a new grandiose scam, losing what money he had, and trusting God (since he often had no other choice). He is so trusting today he even trusts Wally, sends him to the dog track with his numbers and his money.

George never trusted me when I told him about his sleep apnea, his risk of high blood pressure, diabetes. He went to his own doctor to prove how foolish I was, and trusted her when she told him he had an intestinal fungus infection. Through a series of treatments and consultations George finally came to the otorhinolaryngological surgeon (ear, nose and throat specialist) who told him he had sleep apnea. He carefully considered, and decided to have surgery to revise his nose and palate, an attempt to relieve the anoxia and the strain on his heart.

Everything George did, everything the doctors and the nurses did was just fine. The surgery went smoothly. But what "the system" did was utterly disastrous. The "discharge planner" (an ex-nurse who follows the orders of the computer programmed by the insurance industry) determined that he be sent home from the hospital while he was still drugged, bleeding, pained and afraid. The "discharge planner" hadn't the slightest awareness that George would go home to his one room apartment with no phone, no way to call for help, nor did she care. The surgeon and the cardiology consultant hadn't the slightest practical or political power to change the discharge decree. All they could do was request a visiting nurse to check on him at home once a day, while George was afraid he would choke and stop breathing once a minute.

Carl and I came to see George late at night the first full day he had been at home. He said it had taken him two hours to find his shoes, another hour to put them on.

"Is your brain not working right? Have you had a stroke?"

We figured out his brain worked, he was just very, very angry to have been abandoned again, frightened and furious.

"How's your stomach?"

"Hurting. Bad. Here," as he pointed to his epigastrium.

"Have you eaten anything?"

"It took me two hours just to get a drink of water."

We found some yogurt in the refrigerator.

"George, you've had a quarter of a century to practice dealing with resentments. This one can kill you quick. Write about it, now."

"I'm not angry."

"I can go to Jim's, get some cimetidine for you."

"Naw, I'll be okay now. The yogurt helped a little."

"I'll see you in the morning."

The next morning at six he was in an ambulance, spent the day in the emergency room waiting for the surgeon on call. At nine that night the surgeon came, took him to the operating room to oversew his perforated duodenal ulcer. I was relieved; I had thought he had a mesenteric artery thrombosis which would have given him almost no chance to survive.

For the next three months George was in intensive care, unconscious much of the time, flailing in pain. Occasionally he awakened enough to believe he was in hell. He was. He couldn't eat, he couldn't breathe, his heart could hardly pump the blood around his body. He didn't have a chance. Subsequent surgeries to repair the ulcer which was not healing were themselves immediate threats to his fragile life.

I did start writing this story when George was dying again, headed for another hopeless surgery. That's nothing new—we all live on borrowed time. That's called grace. George died several times this year, about the time Jim died, not long after Larry keeled over. George died several times this year, and learned over and over to trust God. Go to the Club and ask him—he'll tell you all about it.

7

God Jobs

I didn't want to believe in miracles. I tried to respect those who did, but I suspected their motivations as unrealistic and self-centered. It seemed to me that people who prayed did it to get things of no inherent value they wanted covetously.

> *"Oh, Lord, won't you buy me a Mercedes-Benz? My friends all drive Porsches; I must make amends."*
>
> —(or something like that)
> from some dead addict, who screamed it
> (I hate to admit I was like that, in my own way)

Only in retrospect could I see that my reluctance to subscribe to miracles was a very thin disguise to cover my wish to be able to explain everything, to control the entire universe in my own mind. I was, indeed, unrealistic and self-centered.

I guess my curiosity as a child, the genesis of my wish to understand and explain things, was honest, as any child's may be. I guess my curiosity had its origins in wonder, in awe, in worshipful respect for what really is. I can't quite recapture childish wonder in my imagination, but I can easily recall the arrogance of the know-it-all. I lived as a know-it-all for decades.

I'm afraid my arrogance predates my memory, for my trust-worthy aunt reported to me that at our first meeting, when I was three, she saw me at the top of a narrow staircase holding a world globe on my shoulder like Atlas. When she exclaimed, "Be careful; you'll fall," I responded haughtily, "I shall not."

I have come to understand miracles not through some brilliant insight, but as a simple bit of common sense. I was reluctant to admit to them, but I may have been too closed, so I considered the possibility of what previously had seemed to me "supernatural" or "paranormal."

I considered the seeming clairvoyant communications between my two brothers (also alcoholics) who are identical twins. They always knew when the other was in trouble, even across the continent. Then I remembered that when we were children I could silently mentally concentrate on a particular card, and my other brother (the normie) would *always* discard it to me. He never won, but I could not easily explain how I did it to him.

When I sobered up I gradually relaxed enough to think in simple terms. (I still don't do it well or often, perhaps, but I *can* do it.) I considered the coincidences which I could not myself explain, conceded even though they occurred rarely, they were real.

As I first admitted I didn't know everything I got a little more comfortable and a little more open, and those puzzling events seemed to become more frequent. It seemed coincidences, especially in relation to people, were fairly frequent. How often I thought of someone and then ran across him, had a dream about a woman and she called soon after, even to wake me from that very dream.

The coincidences became more frequent, I began to open a little more, and I began to realize everything that happens any where, any time is a miracle. It is only my perception of the miracles which is limited, not the reality of them. In fact, every moment of life, every particle of a molecule in relation to every other particle, every vector of energy in the universe is a miracle.

I couldn't make these events happen, and I can't begin to explain most of them. It has taken me most of my life at the end of the Twentieth century to get to the simple truth Job was at about four or five thousand years ago.

THEN THE UNNAMABLE ANSWERED JOB FROM WITHIN THE WHIRLWIND:

Who is this whose ignorant words
     smear my design with darkness?
Stand up now like a man;
     I will question you: please, instruct me.

Where were you when I planned the earth.
Tell me, if you are so wise.

◆   ◆   ◆

JOB SAID TO THE UNNAMABLE:

I am speechless: what can I answer?
I put my hand on my mouth.
I have said too much already;
now I will speak no more.

—from <u>The Book of Job</u>
translated and with an introduction by Stephen
Mitchell
Kyle Cathie, London, 1989

But how well did Job get along with his friends Bildad, Elip-
haz and Zophar? Maybe I'm not doing so badly in that
regard. I do have understanding friends. I may not be real
good at understanding and I know I don't meet all the
expectations or desires of my wife or children or step-chil-
dren or fellows in the Program, but I do live in the real world
with them every day, and that's better than any alternative
(like *not* living or *not* being real).

I get along with my friend Keith very well, I think. We are
very different in the world, but very like each other in the
parts of our souls which are recovering. I think we are to

each other very different from how we have been to most everybody else in our lives.

Much of what we have shared has been in smaller and larger episodes of coincidence, unexplainable things I can remember and report only in a shadowy way. These are things that happen and can be noted, but the fullness is in the being *in* them, and cannot fully be dragged out of a later retelling.

Just when my Jeep Cherokee was repossessed, my father had a stroke and gave up driving. For a dollar my mother sold me his hail-dented old black Chrysler sedan, all power and red plush upholstery. Because of its odd luxurious derelict appearance my children called it "the pimp-mobile." One of my brothers was unemployed in another town, so he had time to drive it to me. For the small price of a one-way plane ticket back where he came from our parents and I got a rare visit with him.

I was sure I would never be able to buy another car, and intended to drive that one until both the Chrysler and I died. Keith helped me keep it running. He came when I called many times, to do what was to him simple, to me impossible.

Once the entire electrical system went dead; nothing worked at all. I called Keith, who said to try to jump-start it and bring it right to him, not to turn it off for any reason. He sounded worried, like he knew the pimp-mobile might be terminal. By the time my daughter and I got it to him, he could find nothing wrong. It started and ran perfectly.

He could not understand it and could not explain it, and he seemed beamingly pleased that the car was okay. My daughter, familiar with previous magical healings of that old car and with the new "spiritual" attitude Keith and I had taken toward daily events, cynically summarized, "Yeah, another God-job." Keith and I nodded in agreement. She goes forward in youth and rationality, and Keith and I just share daily awe as we trust in God together.

Several years ago I got a relatively new luxury sedan from my brother who had just started to sell used cars newly sober (a difficult trick, since to stay sober you have to stay honest). Keith had directed him toward the job at a place where he used to sell used cars himself. I don't know where I got the several thousand dollars and the credit, but it is paid for now, no longer new. I still drive it, and think I will until we both are dead.[9]

One blizzard day I thought I had it all under control. I had checked the weather report and set the clock an hour early so I could get to work on time in the mess it was bound to be. I knew I had a second set of keys on the kitchen shelf, so I went out to the parking lot in my bath robe, started the car and left it running so it would warm up, locked it, went back into the apartment for coffee and to get dressed for work, and really felt in control…until I couldn't find my other set of keys.

Calmly I tried the coat hanger trick, but these new cars are tighter built than the ones we used to steal. I tried every approach, remembering why the second set of keys was not on the kitchen shelf where I thought I had last put them. I had locked my keys in the car while on an A.A. weekend in the mountains and had paid thirty dollars to a locksmith to open it. He had tried the coat hanger and every other trick, and had finally opened it while I was in a meeting—but he wouldn't tell me how. For the next trip I had put the second set of keys somewhere available and safe so that wouldn't happen to me again, but that blizzard morning I could not for the life of me remember where it was I had put them.

I thought of Keith, and tried even harder to be calm and persistent with the coat hanger so I wouldn't have to call him, to inconvenience him, and to admit to him the foolish thing that I had done. But I had to get to work, so finally I gave up my hopeless repetitions and asked for help. I called him.

Keith came soon with his jimmy made out of a hacksaw blade. I was confident it would work. I was happy. It wasn't working, and with every effort from every angle we realized it wasn't going to work that way. I was still happy, because my friend was helping me and we both trusted, and we were confident not in ourselves or even in each other, but in the One whom we had come to know looked out for us each.

When we finished trying, and I had gotten Keith a fresh hot cup of coffee and had called my work to tell them things didn't look real good for getting there on time, Keith turned to me and said,

"Ford key, huh? I've got a Ford key here in my pocket…"

"Not from that van you bought from Mel before he died? What is it, a sixty-three?"

"Not that old. Sixty-five, I think."

"But this is an eighty-nine Thunderbird. A sixty-three utility van can't have the same key."

He sipped his coffee and slipped the old key into the new lock, turned it, looked at me with his head tilted at a funny angle, face down, eyes toward heaven. The door opened. He said "I've just got to see…" and turned off the engine, removed my key, put in Mel's key and started the car right up.

"Another God job?"

"I'll drink to that."

We laughed. I made it to work on time.

We sometimes don't see each other or call for weeks at a time, but when we do it is often simultaneous. That's not such a coincidence; we live in relation to each other whether we talk or not, so why not talk at the same time?

My old drinking buddy who took me to my first meeting shares that kind of relation with me too. For months we will go our different ways; when we do encounter each other it seems by accident but always meets our unidentified reciprocal needs. The morning I got a serious legal notice he came into my office without an appointment; I treated his rash and he gave me a needed legal opinion. Another time he called me with chest pain, I went to his office; he gave me a referral to a lawyer when I needed it, and I explained why he liked a new painting he had chosen without knowing why. He performed my brother's wedding on a day that happened to be his own twenty-fifth anniversary (and later he married me and my very last wife).

Paths cross, and it is no accident. We need each other. Maybe we cross paths because we are on the same path. Every molecule is a miracle, I am sure, and persons are much more complex than molecules. Our relations are more intricate than we can understand. Some of us (like me) analyse the hell out of it, and that's got to be okay; perhaps that comes from normal childish wonder, a form of sanity. Whether we analyse it or not, we need to live it and to accept it. Things will happen the way they should, in the long run, at least on the spiritual plane.

Keith married again a couple years ago. He and Anita tried living together, but it didn't work. She screamingly and absolutely threw him out twenty-three times in two years, so he considered how hopeless the relationship was, asked her to marry him, and she did. Their relationship improved with the commitment from him into which he engaged her reciprocity.

Among the other furniture or baggage which came into the marriage was Anita's perpetually perplexed dependent ex-husband, Howard. He had been Keith's friend for many years, but Keith had not intended to marry or adopt him. Howard had a tree trimming business which needed Keith's responsible attention and energy. Anita had divorced Howard years earlier, but had never completely given up taking care of him, especially in recurring crises when he needed a couch to sleep on, a meal.

One of the biggest sharings for Keith and Anita was in taking care of her mother. The old sick woman had been in a nursing home, but when she came to Keith's and Anita's small apartment for a visit she was so much happier they wanted her to stay, for her sake and for their sense of worth.

They asked Anita's family to help them care for her at their home, to contribute something so they could get a bigger place. Communication in families sometimes is not harmonious. (My clairvoyant brothers do not speak to each other today, and I wasted a half century being spiritually closed or psychically confused toward my two nearest siblings.) The simple goal of caring for Anita's mother was diffused and distracted in petty greeds, jealousies and suspicions.

An agreement was come to through Keith's patience (not saintly, but slowly effective) that the family would help him purchase the little house his own mother was renting, and he would refurbish it for his wife, his mother-in-law and himself.

So, Keith and his wife had shared purpose and harmony, and she moved in with her sister while he slept on the floor of the little house undergoing renovation. It was so for more than a year, during which Anita's mother died in the nursing home.

He knew his wife was ill also, feared if she didn't quit smoking she would not live long. If she had quit smoking she would not have lived long, for the damage had been done long since. When she was in the hospital on a ventilator there seemed little hope, as her lung cancer had rapidly enveloped both her main stem bronchi left and right, and her esophagus. Her family wanted to let her go, to avoid further pain and expense, but Keith stood fast for a trial of radiation to shrink the tumor.

It took a month of painful effort to confirm the cancer was stronger than her ability to live, but I know that month was no loss, for in it Keith gave up his paralysing depression, at least for this time, and confirmed his identity as a trusting and loyal husband, a trusting and loyal child of God.

Keith's example, like the others in this set of stories and in our daily awareness in the Fellowship, sustains me today. I have no more dynamic guide than my real friends who have found a way to live with integrity in a world consumed with self-centered confusion.

Carl had been relapsing and utterly crazy. He had gone from detox to a halfway house in Cheyenne. He did not know why until I asked him and he realized: He had returned to Denver while Anita was in the hospital, helped Keith in his business for a few days, crucial days for the business, not having realized even that Anita was sick, "because God told me to." Still in a cloud Carl drove to California in someone else's car, where he is now safe and recovering again in jail (for taking someone else's car). Tomorrow I'll send him a few dollars for writing paper and a razor.[10]

Fred had been staying at the little house with Keith, slowly and carefully installing the windows Anita wanted, the kitchen tile, and slowly and carefully sobering up again. (Larry had started to help Keith with the construction, but he seemed a bit too scattered then, right at the unanticipated end of his complex life.) Fred couldn't hang on to sobriety this time, nor to the task at hand. He ran a borrowed car into a bridge at sixty miles an hour. He survived, and is recuperating again. Perhaps some day he will walk. Perhaps he will find a way to make amends again to his wife and daughter, to his friend Keith.

When it had become clear how slim Anita's chances were, the goal for all of us became to get her home, to the house she had planned so long, had waited for. It didn't happen exactly that way, but I think it happened; I think Anita is home now in the little house she planned, the house Keith took everything he had to renovate for her.

Perhaps as I walk down any street now, see the undistinguished ordinary dwellings row on row, I will remember that little house. Within it I know are the indelible traces of life and death crises, hopes which are not self-centered unrealistic prayers but only real life in its progress. There the loyalty which transcends death stands fast, like Keith stands forever and patient by the hospital bed, present to his life-and-death partner.

The night he buried her I came to that house to eat cake and visit. The visitors all gone, Keith said we may as well go to a meeting, so we went, together. After the meeting at York Street, coming down the stairs, I saw Keith a few steps ahead of me talking to Matthew, drunk again the many-thousandth time, red-faced and crying, desperate. I knew from seeing.

All the other recovering persons knew from seeing, didn't have to peer or ask, just felt the truth, the harmony as we went from the York Street Club to the place my wife works and tends to drunks wet and sober. Keith and I took Matthew to Pete's Kitchen for his first meal in three days, and Keith took Matthew home to sleep on the floor with himself and Howard and the dogs. Carl would still be living there if he hadn't gone to prison in California to save his life, God's way to get him off the streets to get sober one more time. He may get out next summer.

Miracles do happen. Keith's two daughters each had sons a couple of weeks apart about a year ago. That's ordinary enough, I suppose. The miracle is that they brought the boys to see Keith for the first time about Christmas. It seems a little strange that alcoholics can bond so immediately in an A.A. club or meeting, but families harbor bitternesses indefinitely. Even families can slowly and partially get back together. Very slowly.

Keith had thought he was renovating the house so he could be family with his invalid mother-in-law and his wife, but that wasn't how it worked out. Now it seems more like a rehabilitation center. Matthew is still sober, a miracle indeed, a God job.[11]

8

Jimmy's Second First Step

"We admitted we were powerless over alcohol—that our lives had become unmanageable."

—Step One of the Twelve Steps

I need the timeless present to sketch this story, for I had meant to draft it to give to Jim on his impossible seventy-first belly-button birthday. He had his birthday, but I hadn't written this note yet. He has gone away in the meantime, swam off into the sunset earlier this year, but he is with me and with thousands of others for the duration.

Jim is the only alcoholic I have ever known who had a normal childhood, and it shows. Well, maybe not entirely normal—his dad was an alcoholic, periodic. What is different from most is that his parents really loved him. "If they found me standing over a body holding a smoking gun my mother would say, 'Not my Jim; he couldn't do such a thing,' and my father would say, 'The son of a bitch had it coming anyhow.'" I guess that's normal, at least Jim said it was.

Jim was the product of his cultural and historic context, accidental or at least beyond his control. He was of such an age that he came to serve in the Army in the Second World War in both the European and Pacific theaters. That didn't determine his personality, but colored his perceptions and idioms.

He had grown up while he was in the Army, became a man drinking, whoring and boxing on the team. He loved to swim, and when he was not long out of the service took a job as a life guard in Miami. Jim never had children, and said he was glad of it, but when I heard him tell how he taught kids to swim I was impressed at his genius for teaching and fathering. He used it generously for thousands of newcomers to the Fellowship.

There were many things about him he did not easily acknowledge as manly: his kindness, his generosity, his commonsense perceptiveness which bordered on the intuitive. He probably thought that drinking and fighting and swimming and dancing and making love to women were the main things. The hundreds or thousands of newcomers he helped know better, that there was something deeper in him.

Jim said women were good for just one thing, as I suppose he heard in the Army, but he acted much more humanely than he spoke. He really loved women, except his last wife, and loved each one of them differently.

When Jim first came to York Street he was a hot-shot salesman who had the world by the tail, except he was temporarily missing a few pieces of necessary equipment. He didn't have a suit of clothes, he didn't have a fancy automobile (or any car at all), he didn't have the ability to stay sober for a morning. Those got in the way of being a hot-shot salesman.

Having no place to live and nothing to eat didn't bother him so much.

Jim was just sober when Ray first walked into York Street. Jim Twelfth-stepped Ray, then Ray Twelfth-stepped Jim. Ray admired Jim because he was a hot-shot salesman. Ray was a purchasing agent, a sort of salesman with not quite enough sociopathy to be a hot-shot, too nice a guy.

Jim didn't stay sober long. It wasn't a woman that threw Jim back into drinking, it was his alcoholism; he could do as well or as poorly with a woman drunk or sober, they didn't drive him or seduce him to drink. Jim and Ray tried to keep each other sober for a couple of years, relapsing in tandem. They were so much alike they nearly killed each other, but they never really had a fist-fight because, as Ray has always known, Jim would have won drunk or sober.

Ray still had a home and family. He remembers Jim crashing on their couch, drinking again, none the less attending to the children, playing with them, running around the yard for hours with them sweating and exerting physically to an extent Ray couldn't do sober. Ray always admired Jim's athletic capacity.

Jim left Denver for San Francisco. He doesn't remember exactly when or why, but probably for the apparition of a job, a "geographic cure." What he does remember is his work with a sponsor, his own conscious presence at meetings. It was then at a meeting he heard someone say, "I'm Jim, and I'm a successful alcoholic." Shocked to hear it, he turned around to see who had spoken, and realized it was himself. He knew immediately what he had meant, that ex-hot-shot with no suit of clothes again, no car, living in a dirty little room without prospects for a next meal, he was successful any day he was sober. It was a new meaning of success which stuck with him for the duration.

His sponsor Jack seemed successful, living in a luxury high-rise. As Jim visited him in his expensively furnished apart-ment, Jack asked him,

"Do you have faith?"

Jim wondered what he meant.

Jack went on, "How do you know that your little room down there hasn't caught fire? Where are all your posses-sions now?"

"I don't think I have much to lose."

"How about your life? What if there were an earthquake? Why are you sitting here acting comfortable in this death-trap? Don't you see, there is no way for you to pro-tect yourself?"

Jim pondered that.

He worked on his inventory, Fifth-stepped it with Jack. The most sensitive item was his first sexual encounter, a gang-bang when he was an adolescent. Jim explained to Jack that all those years he had carried guilt about exploiting the girl who was considered the village punch-board.

"What do you think you did that was so wrong?"

"I defiled her."

"No. All the other guys had already done that, and that's what she seemed to want at the time, for her own reasons. What really happened?"

"I tried to kiss her, and she wouldn't let me."

"Now, that is something uncomfortable, indeed. Everyone else came to screw her, and she let them, but you wanted to *kiss* her!"

"It was the most uncomfortable rejection of my life, I think."

"Sure it was, because you were at cross-purposes with her, trying to be romantic. You owe an amend for that one."

Jack taught Jim a simple technique for doing the Fourth Step; Jim called it a fifth column. Everyone who works the Twelve Steps knows the first column is simply a list of the persons, institutions or ideas that make you angry. The second is simply to state what those parties did to hurt you. The third is to divine what part of you was hurt (which experience shows us to be a boringly limited list: self-esteem, security, ambitions, and personal and sexual relations). The fourth column (on the traditional yellow legal pad scrawled with the stub of a Number Two pencil) is not clearly illustrated in the example in the Big Book on page 65, but is clearly referred to a couple of pages later (page 67) to answer the question, "What was my part in this?" (that is, how did I provoke it, invite it, prolong it?).

Jack's fifth column is "What was my motivation?" Jim found it very helpful in that first instance, and many thereafter, to honestly assess his own motivations and how they might vary from those of the persons he encountered. It helped him close sales quite effectively (as a sober salesman, no longer a hot-shot, but a man working to be of service to the customer and the boss) to honestly acknowledge to himself that his motivation was to get his commission and the customer's motivation was to get something worthwhile for his dollars.

Jim did get sober, finally. As with us all, it was the disease that beat him, and he couldn't get better until he was licked. He managed to stay sober even when he got involved in some not-so-legitimate sales jobs, like when he was vice president of Micky Mouse Airlines (capitalized on an American Express card). He came to know when his motivations were verging on dishonesty, and found the humility to back away.

Jim spent more than thirty years at the York Street Club, was the manager three different times, knew the ups and downs of his own alcoholism and the irrationality of a community of alcoholics trying to stay sober together. But that community, erratic though it was, had a daily reliable consistency for him, reliable practical steps which he could use every day to stay alive and sober, other persons who shared those simple principles, as well as the certainty that someone was going to act goofy, that things in the world and in the Club would never be quite serene.

One day Jim sat at the "million dollar table[12]" in the Club Café with a half a dozen beautiful women. One, his former girlfriend, looked at him and said, "I'll bet you'd like to make love to every woman at this table." He sat silently and smiled benignly, thinking to himself, "And I have, my dear, I have."

Jim and I met at the bridge table in the lounge. He had little patience for my "creative bidding," seemed to think at least one thing in the world should follow predictable rules, the game of bridge. There was no animosity between us, but our close friendship only could take place when we had over-come the obstacle of my deficient bridge-playing.

I knew he was worried about his prostate, but he had diffi-culty addressing that problem in action. It was more than merely bothersome to him, more than mere urinary urgency, for it had rendered him impotent, had interfered in the joy of loving women which he had done so well for so long. He feared he would die of prostate cancer, but would not talk about it. He ruminated.

When our friend Bob began to urinate blood Jim encour-aged me to talk with him about it, and I tried. Despite a quarter of a century of sobriety, Bob relapsed agonizing over his bladder cancer. That got Jim's attention, and let him level with me about his fears. He got a test at the VA Hospital, and it seemed his prostate was okay. He had trouble believing it, but gradually cheered up. He still played good bridge and mediocre golf. Jim developed a golf scoring system just for old men who didn't play so well; instead of reporting, "I shot five over par," or "I had three birdies," he would simply hold up fingers indicating "One," or "Two," his total number of pars for the round—birdies and bogies didn't count.

We got along fine as friends, and got closer as the months and years went on, sometimes playing golf together serious and skilless. Jim's first clue that something was not right with him came on the golf course. Even though his swing was much more conservative than my wild flailing, one day teeing off he fell down on the follow-through. His tremor had been getting worse, so that he could hardly hold a hand of cards, and now his coordination was unreliable. That was quite a blow to the macho athlete, especially so early in the golf season.

Then one day there was that little lump on his chest wall he raised his shirt to show me in Seth's office (the room where the pinball machine is which I have used often for quick physical examinations.) I knew that was a lymph node from his lung cancer, and before we left that little room I made sure he knew that was a likelihood, but not a certainty.

Ray and Jim had always been spiritual brothers. Jim knew Ray was having all the signs of prostate disease, and was worried for him. Ray went in for a blood test, which was not normal. Jim asked me what it meant. I told him it meant Ray probably had prostate cancer. Jim's response was in action, not analysis. He went to the VA for the examination he had been avoiding, to show Ray the way of straight-forward braveness.

It didn't take long that spring to figure out that Jim had several large tumors in his brain, most likely from a lung cancer which was rapidly growing and spreading. I was glad we had really been friends before he got sick, because I knew this was likely to be a painful downhill process, that Jim needed me as his friend knowledgeable in medicine, not as his doctor.

He asked me what would happen, and I honestly tried to tell him I couldn't predict, and neither could his doctors. He pressed me daily. I admitted the likely expectations were that his now mild neurologic symptoms, tremor and imbalance, would get worse, not better. I leveled with him that paralysis or seizures would likely enough occur, but whatever happened I would be there.

He was always unconsciously on the lookout for chances to be generous without looking or feeling charitable. He asked Colette to do him a favor, to drive him sometimes where he needed to go, since he could not well drive himself. She could use his car; in fact she could just let him sign the title over to her, but he would pay the insurance premiums since he already had the policy. (He wasn't very subtle about giving the car to someone who needed it.)

Jim and I agreed his young doctors at the VA were generally good people (except one surgeon with a German name and a Prussian attitude whom Jim called "Herr Doktor Mengele"), but he wanted me with him to translate doctor talk or to protect him, so I struggled with my ego and my discomfort in institutions. I tried to lay back, and thanks to the help of his other friends, especially Sue (whose mother died sober this year also) and Ray (who is still sober), we shared the blessed tasks.

Jim had hundreds of friends, dozens who asked about him every day, but only a few could come to see him. I got a clear understanding of that common limitation, especially from Larry. We ran into each other at the club, sat in the lounge to have coffee. It was just after Thanksgiving last year.

"Your children and grandchildren were here. How was your visit?"

"Wonderful, just wonderful. I had to pawn my golf clubs to get groceries, but, oh, what a feast we had. It's a miracle, after all the years we didn't communicate, after I left, after their mother stopped speaking *to* me, only *about* me."

"I know what you mean. Been there, done that."

"You're not a grandfather, Nathan. You're missing the spiritual part."

"Oh, I look forward to it, when and if it happens."

"How's Jim?"

"He's fine. Why don't you ask him? He's a whole three blocks away. Here's his phone number…"

"No, I can't call him right now."

"Afraid?"

"I wouldn't want to linger like that. I just can't see him. When *I* go, I want to go just like that. I don't mind dying, but I couldn't stand it to last so long."

"Get over that fear, Larry. Jim may be going soon, and you'll want to say goodbye. Hell, any of us may be going soon."

A old girlfriend of Jim's who saw him slipping physically said, "If I were in your spot I'd never draw another sober breath." Neither he nor I said much, just nodded. When she left we shared the obvious, that she probably wouldn't, but he would, draw every sober breath left to him. We agreed we were grateful that she had said that so blatantly; it confirmed for us that our sobriety (and our friendships in it) were all we had, and it was enough. No, we wouldn't willingly give that up, not even in the face of pain or fear.

I had a strong impression about how panicked Jim was in the face of a prospect of increasing dependence and pain, that none of us could face such things well, but that we needed him to continue to teach us how to play with the cards life dealt us. I acknowledged, especially as he made his suicide contingency plans, that he could make a quick exit. But I begged him not to be so fast and efficient about it because I knew we were all slow and thick, needed time to catch on. In his confirmation of his powerlessness over his mortality, I begged Jim to show us the way.

We talked openly and bluntly about what to do, agreed that Jim would stay in his own apartment as long as he could, finish in the VA hospice if necessary, that there would be plenty of medication if he had any pain, that he would leave the details to Skippy (or Charlie or whatever that higher power's name might be), not kill himself, not get drunk on purpose.

We discussed spiritual matters, but couldn't do it without a sense of humor (for we were convinced God has no other reason to concern Herself with us except as a joke). We formulated a new-old cult, the Radical Primitive Pre-Biblical Jews. Jim's being an Irish Catholic was no problem in our cult; we had room for anyone who wanted to join us. We considered ourself the "choosing" rather than the "chosen" people. We discovered our motto was "Phuq'm," very ancient pseudo-Hebrew which liberally translated means, "Let God do it." We were glad just to be sober.

Jim wanted a simple cheap quick disposal, like our Jewish hero Moses who was tossed unceremoniously into an anonymous cave. While he could still walk we went to Feldman's, the neighborhood Jewish funeral parlor. The proper demeanor of the young salesman was at first unruffled. He addressed me politely, the one in the suit and tie, but I silently deferred to Jim.

"I'm the corpse in this operation."

"Of course. How can I help you?"

"What's cheapest and quickest?"

"We have a number of elegant secure caskets."

"Who needs secure? I mean, is it cheaper to be put in the ground or incinerated?"

"We have inexpensive pine caskets in the next room I can show you."

"Can I try one on for size?"

The young fellow caught on and lightened up after a bit. Jim's humor put most everyone at ease, even those who at first were too stodgy to appreciate his lusty irreverence.

He didn't have time or patience for some sorts of things, especially the IRS, and especially before noon. A call came at nine AM, to which he responded in a most businesslike manner,

> "Ms. Aguilar of the IRS, is it? Well, let me tell you three things: first, I'm dying of cancer; second, I don't take calls before noon; third, I don't have any money, and if I did I wouldn't give any to you; and another third, come to think of it, you can all go straight to hell."

Click. He hung up the phone, looked at me with an impish grin and said, "I always wanted to say that to the IRS, and now I've done it."

We made plans for his eventual demise, that we would go to the tattoo parlor the next day to prepare for it. When he passed away I was to have the television crews ready at the nearest IRS office to document my dumping his naked corpse on the front steps, the message inscribed across his buttocks, "You wanted my ass—now you've got it." He eventually decided to be cremated and tossed into the Pacific Ocean.

Jim had increasing trouble making it up the steps to the Club, increasingly stayed at home sitting in his reclining chair listening to Pavarotti. I developed little missions, tasks I could accomplish with difficulty, like finding a Jeannette MacDonald CD for him to listen to. Those missions let me feel competent, a little bit important, alive. The simplest tasks for me were never simple. Getting a vibrating pillow for his back took three trips to the drug store.

Most every day I went to the Oven, Jim's overheated one room apartment. (None of us ever thought to call it Hell, perhaps because it was all that was left of the world he lived in, none of us ever thought for a moment he deserved any punishment, and for him eighty-five degrees was just comfortable.) Sometimes I was intrusive and brash, sometimes subdued and defeated, but almost every day I went: Jim was my sex and table tennis sponsor.

"I can't be your ping pong sponsor; I don't know the first thing about ping pong."

"You don't know anything about sex, either; that's why I trust you."

He fumed. (He knew plenty about sex. One of his many girlfriends proposed getting him a set of satin sheets with names embroidered of all the women he had ever made love to; then she quickly considered the full names would take up too much space and asked him to settle for just the initials.)

We teased each other. I loved him more each day. I loved that scrawny old salt "Captain York" (embroidered in gold braid on the yachting cap a friend got him for his birthday, an ironic moniker for an old Army boxer who had pummeled many sailors in Tokyo bars, no doubt, but appropriate to the A.A. Club senior statesman.)

Increasingly he was limited to his chair, had to hold the walls to make it the few feet to the bathroom. We feared the pain which likely would come, and the progressive growth of tumor. They did come, but they went away also, the miracle of real life. The doctor in me wanted to prepare him for the inexorable demise and was surprised when the worst continually and repeatedly never came; the friend in me never doubted he would live his whole life, which he did. I learned again to prefer to be the friend.

Jim's one overwhelming fear was of pain; the doctor in me knew it was likely that he have intolerable and continual pain in his head, in his chest wall, difficulty breathing, seizures. Pain in his hip came suddenly and sharply, what should have been progressively increasing pain from invasion of cancer into his bone; it didn't progress, but receded. Pain in his back remained a problem, especially as increasingly he could do nothing but sit.

Had the oncologist been reluctant to promise Jim ample pain medication I think he would have suicided early in this year of growth just to maintain a semblance of control in the face of fear, but she was adamant that he would not be allowed to suffer even if he wished to.

His feet swelled badly, the right more than the left. He could hardly walk. We had to improvise shoes. He and I were proud of me when I managed deftly to extend the latchet of his sandal with a wire coat hanger. It worked for the duration.

Tumor again erupted through his chest—and then abated. Lymph nodes blew up in his right armpit and his groin, then discontinued expanding. The parallel enlargement of the tumor in his lungs never choked off his air. Terrible pain came in his abdomen—then responded to simple medications, although his appetite never returned. He made efforts to drink a small can of Ensure once or twice a day.

He wasted away physically over the next months, but not spiritually. Radiation treatment to his brain did away with his hair, but instead he was adorned by a bushy white beard. He looked the same to me each day, but to everyone else completely transformed. He had changed from the robust "Moose" to a crusty little sea captain.

He grumbled some to me, but generally he sparkled, paid attention to others, really cared how they fared, understood their foibles. Those on whom he most depended he scrutinized carefully, criticizing only the little things (but that with vigor) like poor judgement in choosing flavors of Ensure. On the phone he was animated, carried on many conversations every day, turning the "How are you?" question around to find out how they were, to help them feel better.

Jim anchored in his recliner and Diana on the other end of the line with *her* lung cancer spread to *her* brain, they had phone sex. I think of them in heaven now, free to do anything they wish, having phone sex with each other, laughing for eternity.

Jim had sexualized relations with every woman he had ever known, at least in fun or fantasy, and he let a little playful love come in for Cathy, the oncologist (those "If I were forty years younger" sorts of comments) and he saved some such play for Cathy's nurse. I had to steer clear of those games; separating roles of friend and doctor can be tricky. But Jim's sexuality was one of the healthiest and most wholesome joys of his life, and our loving friendship brought out mine.

I couldn't care for him daily, run errands for him, think of him, listen to Jeannette MacDonald with him without sharing a feeling for Jim's powerful sexuality. We had many beautiful women friends in the program almost all of whom I had maintained "platonic" relations to, but gradually and unconsciously, under Jim's influence, I converted some of those to what I would call "Socratic," shared it with him tacitly and discretely, only in a smile between us.

By August Jim was too weak to come to the Club, so we had his thirtieth A.A. birthday in the party room of his apartment house. Several dozen old-timers and newcomers were there to tell salty tales about Jim, boldly risqué jokes (especially from the women), to eat cake and ice cream. It was just another A.A. meeting with several hundred years of continuous sobriety sitting gleefully in one room; we have about a thousand such meetings a week in our town.

Autumn came, quiet noisy days for me, as Jim blessed my physical and spiritual union with the most beautiful and unmanageable of all the women he and I knew. Angela and I were there at Jim's apartment every day, seeing each other in passing, often, as I was coming from my work, she going to hers. Our private domestic trivia and business were at home with Jim. His mediation and advice were welcome, especially the paternal aegis of his wisest-ever axiom for me, "Don't ever analyse yourself out of a good piece of ass."

Winter set in and Jim dwindled stubbornly. In January he reached his seventy-first birthday, relieved that his only close relative, his Aunt Ruth, had given up the ghost before him, she ninety-four. He had feared the impact of his own death on her, had he predeceased her, to lose her little Jim. Jim cried tenderly that his cousin Dick would think to send him the cross from her casket, since he could not attend her funeral. He hung it on the wall between the gold-framed pictures of his parents.

It had been most of a year. He had gone further than was conceivable and was still with us. It was like swimming the English Channel and exhausted reaching shore, turning with an impish grin to go back again and make it a round trip. Ray and I nodded with Aunt Ruth, agreed the kid was a real champ.

Finally he was so insubstantial he couldn't easily throw his weight back into the recliner, because he had too little weight. Worse, he was too weak to disengage the recliner, and was stuck like a turtle on its back. Time came to go to the hospital again, headed for the hospice. Those days were short, his breathing heavy, consciousness waning, friends brought by God for last moments, fingertips waving, whispered goodbyes.

9

Howard the Hero

Sixty-six years old this very day, still climbing trees. Maybe this is the essence of being human, above all to be simian, to be able to climb trees. Prehensile thumbs are necessary to us, and maybe prehensile tails also. Oh, let us mourn the atrophy of our prehensile tails.

Built like a gorilla, grey and white hair shooting out in all directions from his mustache, from under his faded plaid cap, Old Silver-Back lumbers silently to the chess table to do silent violence against another secretly cerebral brute, chessboard gladiators they. Any chess opponent is real somehow to Howard, their relation passionately mortal. Each silently yearns for some small symbolic victory in a life in which he has long since given up hope of winning. They lost their tails long ago in evolution (and lost their asses many times during their own lifetimes).

Howard looks rough and grunts gruffly in monosyllables, but at home or in his truck (which often serves as his home) the classical music station is tuned in, turned loud so he can hear it. Perhaps this is reminiscence of the promising young flautist, a serious student of classics and other intellectual matter whose early dissipation took him too soon to look at the world *up* from the gutter of skid row, *down* only from the tops of trees, lonely, a comic King Kong.

"Chopper" to the tree-trimming trade, we call him "chain-saw head" because he can't hear anything you say (unless you whisper something derogatory about him from across the room), I hope Howard is not within earshot now, for he always misunderstands my love and admiration for his imperfectness, takes my candid statements as criticisms.

I consider Howard is a mirror for myself, like all the others I have met in sobriety. Through our fellowship we have gone beneath the surface on which we appear different; we have met in a special human commonality where there is only the need to get sober and to stay sober in order to live. Honesty, willingness and openness are the bases of the change in attitude which lets us live together on borrowed time; so I think Howard should be tolerant of my verbal gruffness, honesty, mere candor.

As I reflect on Howard it occurs to me that he is a master of progressive isolation. It is not only his acquired deafness, nor is it merely his occupational isolation in the tops of trees, but it is a gradually progressing spiritual aloneness which he spontaneously acknowledges and cherishes. I imagine him like an old weathered boat, encrusted in barnacles which are themselves encrusted in barnacles. Because I look from outside of him I see his shape clearly enough, but he is surprised when I read what is obvious. Like the child who closes his eyes and believes the world can no longer see him, we who isolate from the mainstream of human intercourse believe we appear no different from all the others, but (alas) we are wrong again.

A talented alert adolescent flautist playing in the symphony or marching band indeed must be exactly in step with the others, exactly in rhythm with the director. Even though he plays his own instrument, the part written by the composer for its unique voice, he must be exactly with the others, and so I know Howard was once. But also I know the sickness which takes us each away, the sliding by of decades without our knowing it, the discrepancy between the kind and orderly person I meant to be and the disruptive discordant drunk I became.

It was not easy for Larry and me to approach Howard (a few weeks before Larry died) but we had to do it then, for we do love him and he was headed for trouble, lumbering again silently toward the precipice, blind and deaf to danger. We drove together to Howard's place, kidnapped him. We took him to Annie's Café close by to feed him supper, talk with him straight, whether it was uncomfortable or not for him or for each of us. Characteristically, and idiosyncratically, Howard confusedly misunderstood that Larry and I were in need of a free meal, and although he was impecunious (as usual) he dug into his pocket to see if he had enough money to feed us all three, or at least Larry and me.

How could we tell him of our concerns? He was being
evicted from his room again to live in his truck; he paid no
attention to the cards or the bids or the rules when we played
pinochle together, and no one wanted to be his partner; he
was hurting Keith's already marginal business by making
bids below cost, and with his irritable ranting running off the
young men who might make good workers for the business
he himself had started many years earlier.

We tried to tell him it was not a question of whether he had
already become intoxicated, or even thought of it. It was his
distance, his spaciness, his being out of harmony with his
friends and the simple needs of his own life—his madness.
We knew it to be deadly, sooner rather than later, and we
care about him, about this person who is our friend, the
whole person, not just appearances, not just the source of a
free meal. We were clumsy, but we persisted. He resisted,
said he hadn't had a drink in over twenty years, so why were
we questioning his sobriety. We tried to understand together
what spiritual sobriety is, what none of the three of us had
ever mastered nor ever will.

I don't know what Howard thought of his little supper meeting with Larry and me, but it was not many weeks later I had
supper with Howard again, this time at Pete's Kitchen. That
was almost exactly a year ago, the day after Howard's sixty-
fifth birthday, December 12, 1995, the day Larry died.

The word got around the club almost instantly, and I got a
page at work, knew almost immediately after it had hap-

pened that Larry had collapsed (was being carried to the same hospital in which Big George was destined to spend a next three months thereafter).

The afternoon became hectic for me, for all of us. I called Larry's children in Omaha to let them know his friends were there to help, so they wouldn't have to rush in panic to care for his possessions and affairs. I called Keith as soon as I could; we met at the Club, agreed our priorities were to take care of Howard and Larry's cat Savage.

We knew Howard had been with Larry when he collapsed, that Larry hadn't made it through the day alive (but through almost sixteen years sober). We were worried that Howard would go out and get loaded, or wander off away from the friends with whom he needed to share mourning and reminiscence, that he might do something foolish or destructive.

We weren't so worried about Savage becoming emotionally unstable or behaviorally deranged, just hungry and lonely. Among my phone calls was one to the manager of Larry's apartment, to let her know we were coming to get the cat. She told us she would stay late, that we should not rush through evening traffic. She was not hesitant to wait for Larry's sake, for Savage's. She had liked them both for years.

Keith and I drove to the place Howard was living, but he was not there. I formulated a detailed but diplomatic note urging him to page me, was attaching it to the door when he drove up. He was carrying a bag of groceries, calm; it was obvious he was not going crazy, just caring for himself and his cats.

Keith, Howard and I in the car rushing through traffic to keep the manager from waiting, caught up with the highlights of the day. I acknowledged I continued to be frustrated with the federal government and the agency for which I did contract work, but as that was the only work available to me I would accept it. Keith, described tree work with the crew separate from Howard (whom Keith left to work alone). That day he had had to take a tearful frustrated Carl out of a cottonwood tree.

"Cottonwoods are frightening. You think you can handle them, looking from the ground, but once you climb up into one everything changes. It is too big. You freeze," Howard explained to me.

"Carl is so egotistic, so belligerent; that's why we call him Howard Junior. He told me he could handle it, so I left him there a half hour or so before I brought him down."

"I took you out of a cottonwood once, Keith, scared and crying."

"I may have been scared, Howard, but I wasn't crying. I never cried in my life except at my wives."

"And how was your day, Howard?"

Larry had been down on his luck, was involved in the usual frustrations of his free-lance construction business (impending law suits both directions), so Howard asked him to meet for breakfast and do some light work with him through the day (a way to give Larry a few dollars). They had finished the tree job at two o'clock, went to the truck, and Larry had collapsed on the sidewalk. Howard yelled for help, did what he could. The ambulance came, but Larry didn't make it. Implying the drama of watching his friend collapse and die, Howard spoke the concrete facts flatly and bluntly.

All those facts were routine in my eyes, I so used to death and dying. What I am in the dark about, I think, is living. I fear we all are in the dark about living, some more densely than others. The being-together as friends of which I came to get a glimpse that afternoon has left me a little wiser about what living really is or can be, and for that I thank Howard especially.

The world of time and space changed for us at the moment of crisis of friends. Keith and I sought Howard, fearing his suffering and disintegration. Fate brought him to us by means we could not have anticipated. We went on together, bereft of our friend Larry, acknowledging our loss, knit together to save the survivor Savage.

We went to the large circular apartment building from which Larry had that morning left alive, rang the bell of the manager's office, got the key to Larry's apartment. The manager had joined us spiritually, awaited purposefully our arrival after her usual hour of closing, Savage and Larry on her heart, she willing to be of service, projecting her strength as well east to Omaha, to Larry's surviving children and grandchildren.

We walked the circle, took the elevator, as each of us often had before, as all of us together had before for pinochle games. The key worked easily. We feared Savage would run and hide. Howard had the foresight to bring a cat-carrier to make the passage easier. (Howard? Foresight? How strange.)

Savage came to greet us. We told him Larry was dead, that he would have to come with us now, that we would care for him as best we could. He went into the small carrier without resistance. The four of us took a last look about the apartment, to rescue valuables for Larry's children, to say good-bye.

We locked the door, walked the circle. We descended to the first floor, knowing we must come to the office eventually. Savage shat and puked, a not unfamiliar feline mode of emotional expression. We took that in stride, experienced cat people each. We walked the circle, but no hallway or office came to us.

Each of us was aware—and each of us was aware each of us was aware—that the physical world was distorted for us. We walked on in the circle much further than the circle could be, no office, no front lobby.

"Does this seem weird to you?"

"Yes. We should have found the office two circles ago."

"Four grown men lost in a small building."

"It's a cottonwood tree! We're caught in a spiritual cottonwood tree!"

Too many times around, but we came eventually to the office, returned the key, thanked the manager and headed back to the middle of town. Savage was fine in the back seat, just smelled bad from vomit and diarrhea. We took him to Howard's place and went for supper.

"At breakfast Larry seemed so well to me," Howard said, rubbing his head and brow. "We met for breakfast the same as we had so often these last fifteen years. He seemed calm, even though I knew he had plenty of problems. You know, it wasn't two weeks ago he saw I was running out of gas and gave me his last eleven dollars. That's the kind of friends we were. We didn't talk about it much, but I really loved that man."

"That's the kind of friends we all are, Howard. Remember a few weeks ago when Larry and I kidnapped you to eat dinner? It was for you, and for Keith; you are both our friends, and you were hurting each other. We had to respond, we had to give you something whether you wanted it or not."

"Yes, Larry and I were friends ever since he came to this town. Lately he has been so frustrated. I was worried he was broke. I only had him working on the ground for me today to give him some money so it wouldn't seem like charity. It wasn't hard work, not so much to kill him, was it? I can do these little jobs by myself if I have to. I've done it for thirty years. Besides, I like the company. Oh, not just anybody, but Larry."

"He was my friend too, Howard, from the first time I came into the Club. We had coffee there not a month ago. He told me he couldn't stand to linger, that when he went he wanted it to be instantaneous. I don't know if he was right to wish that, but he got his wish today. God bless him."

"He looked so well this morning. I thought somehow he was relieved of the things that had worried him the last few months. I saw his hair, you know his hair, straight, white, all in place. I saw the yellow glow from underneath the white, golden almost, like what it must have been like when he was young. And his posture, erect; Larry always stood tall."

"It was his back, Howard. His back hurt, so he had to stand ram-rod straight."

"I remember this morning, seeing him as if I had never seen him before, his hair, his stature, hearing the tone of his voice—not the words so much, just the music."

"Ah, that's it, Howard. You saw and heard the real man this morning, and it was no accident. Congratulations, Howard, you were alive and aware this morning."

"You're a medical man, Nathan. Tell me what I should have done."

"From what you tell me, Howard, Larry was dead before he hit the ground. You couldn't have revived him."

"But what could I have done better? Maybe he could be alive. I saw him rub his shoulder, then look funny and fall, his face almost purple, right there on the sidewalk beside the truck. I ran to him, thumped him on the chest, blew air in his mouth. What should I have done?"

"You did what you should have done, Howard; you were present for your friend this morning, open to who he really was."

Larry had told me just after Thanksgiving that he couldn't stand to linger like Jim was doing, that he wanted to go in a moment. That Tuesday afternoon he did go, so quickly I am convinced he was dead before he hit the ground. Ironic though it may seem, Jim lived on into January, into another year on the calendar, into his own seventy-second.

December twelfth Howard had breakfast with Larry, then supper with me. It was a remarkable day for him. I don't know how it changed him, exactly, for he seems much the same, still lives and works marginally with Keith, sleeps on Keith's floor again.

Howard was a hero not for rushing to save a falling man, but for opening his eyes and seeing, at least once. Our life is blinding and confusing mostly; moments of clarity are precious, should be shared freely.

A few days ago, at our most recent pinochle game, Howard brought a ragged deck of cards, reminded us that was the very deck with which Larry played his last game. When we finished playing he put the deck in his cap. I told him to take them home and frame them. I think he has done that, as playing with that deck on the anniversary of Larry's death seemed a religious ritual, memorial of a rare close friendship.

10

A Posthumous Meeting

We jokingly projected we would be with Larry again on his seventeenth A.A. birthday, January eleventh. All jokes are serious, and even though we meant it in good humor we didn't for a moment disbelieve Larry would be there, still sober, still somewhat sour, fun-loving too. Any time we go to a meeting we carry with us all the people we have met along the way, all the way back to Bill Wilson and Doctor Bob Smith. When there are just two persons sitting at an A.A. meeting, millions are present. We are not alone.

A birthday meeting for Larry was a warm private joke to us, but young Jed took it seriously. He called me, asked how we could have some sort of memorial for Larry. Jed is not one of us, not an alcoholic, but he had worked with Larry and immediately had felt toward him as if Larry were his loving father, accepting his faults, guiding him to do better.

I told Jed to call Chuck, the manager of the Club, to ask him if we could schedule the use of a meeting room for Larry's birthday. Jed made all the arrangements, helped us contact Larry's children in Nebraska and Iowa, arranged their airplane reservations. He even had flowers on the table for the meeting (not so unusual for a birthday, and a little like a funeral). Jed brought Inez, the wife he was then preparing to divorce. (Perhaps they are still together because of the spiritual glue they encountered at Larry's birthday meeting.)

I didn't have to organize or manage a thing. I sat at the back of the room and watched friends and strangers come in to sit around the table. Larry's grown children came to town just for the meeting, proper, quiet, a little edgy. A few people chatted quietly, a few busied themselves getting cups of coffee and ash trays. It began a bit subdued for an A.A. meeting.

Jed had organized it all, but he didn't know how to run an A.A. meeting. He thought I would do it, but I was too comfortable sitting and watching, and I was afraid all my words would get in the way of Larry's birthday. I told Jed not to worry, that there were a few more minutes before we were to start, that God would provide the ram (get someone to chair).

Keith walked in at exactly seven o'clock. The only place left at the table was right in front, where the chairperson usually sits. I guided my friend Keith with my left eyebrow, saying, in effect, "It's yours." He looked back at me, that big strong silent slow-talking dark mustachioed giant, shook his head. I pointed at the book; reluctantly he took it and started the meeting. I thought I had helped Jed get off the hook, egotistically still managing everything, silent as a mime.

Keith started the meeting matter-of-factly, his calm bass voice lifting fifty or so fidgeting people into a focused calm congregation. After the Serenity Prayer he handed the book to Jed who sat next to him, asked him to read the beginning of Chapter 5, "How It Works." Only then did I realize Jed, one of the few in the room unfamiliar with that passage with which we alcoholics open most every meeting, could hardly read. Trusting God a little, I sat and listened.

I could have taken charge a few weeks earlier, could have rattled off "How It Works" by memory, but for once I was intent on letting God run the show. I think my relative calm, passivity and uncharacteristic serenity was all for Larry, quite personally. I didn't care about the facts, that he was dead. I only thought of what my friend needed, the same as we had done for each other for years. He had keeled over from a heart attack because he was too up tight, especially about money. He died trying silently to control a stubborn universe. What my friend needed was relief from habitual internal grandiosity and furor; he needed some serenity, so I had to be serene for his sake.

I sat back and listened, and heard. I listened to Jed plod through the reading, the condensed statement of the Twelve Steps, the "ABC's" ("I can't, He can, I think I'll let Him"). His slowness helped me listen anew to the heart of the Program which had saved me. His deliberateness helped me hear solid meaning in the simple statements.

I heard many persons speak, every one of them directly to each other and to Larry. I was able to sit without speaking for a long time (a minor miracle). I was not surprised when the hour had gone by and the meeting continued, for this time there was no hurry; this was taking place in human spiritual reality, not in mere time and space.

Jed spoke early, maybe first. He said a few simple words about how Larry had encouraged him and guided him when they had worked jobs together. Larry made no secret to Jed that his own life had been turned around in Alcoholics Anonymous, but he didn't try to get Jed to stop drinking or to stop anything. Larry just shared openly with Jed the changes of attitude he had himself come to gradually over years of growth, especially to avoid anger and judgementalness. Larry never told Jed not to divorce Inez, didn't try to patch a family secretly to satisfy his own ego. Jed's mourning for his friend, his sincere and grateful voice and face, told us as much as his words of appreciation.

Grateful Annie remembered Larry for his politeness and respect for women. When she was new he had not "hit on" her, had not tried to "Thirteenth Step" her. He was reserved toward new women, encouraged them to get and stay sober one day at a time, did not intrude on their vulnerability like some men did. (Of course he talked a lusty game with us friends at the pinochle table, but he never acted rapacious toward women.)

Gordon said something similar, that Larry was always sincere and honest, cheerful toward people in the Club, in the Program, especially accepting toward newcomers. Gordon had not known him well, but remembered and cherished ordinary conversations with Larry, especially about the Program and the Fellowship, life and God, and baseball.

The manager of a fancy restaurant famous for its pulchritudinous dancers spoke of Larry's politeness and respect for the women who worked there. It was a sincere encomium, but it occurred to me that since Larry liked the food and the dancers but did not drink, he may have been one of the few regular customers who was not drunk and disorderly. That made it easier for the dancers and manager to like him, no doubt.

Hank recalled Larry's organization and coaching of championship York Street softball teams. Others remembered his serving as the Club's social organizer for holiday dances.

One after another many people spoke honestly the most complimentary reflections of Larry. It was no surprise when several close friends, including Greg (a sometime partner on remodeling jobs) began to point out some of Larry's idiosyncrasies and weaknesses. In the most uncritical ways they remembered some episodes of his irritability and stubbornness. They were helping us remember and love Larry in a more realistic way, painting him as human, sometimes faulty.

Most striking of what was said was what wasn't said. There was a presence we all became aware of, a reality presented to us by the youngest person there, Donovan, then just one year old. Helen had come, the woman Larry was married to for a short time earlier in their recoveries. I knew they had been married, that they were each at the Club often, that they were friendly toward each other, and I didn't need to know more. Diane was there, Helen's daughter, Donovan's mother. We had cheered her through her pregnancy with him, welcomed him as we often welcome infants hatched at York Street.

Helen spoke briefly of her respect for Larry, the friendship they shared years after they found they could not sustain that marriage earlier in their recoveries. She asked Diane to speak, Diane who had been self-conscious about being present at all, much less to speak.

> "I didn't know if I could say anything at this meeting for Larry, knowing his real children were going to be here. Larry was my stepfather for a short time during my childhood, but he was the only real father I ever had. He always cared about me and encouraged me. When Donovan was coming along, especially when he was born, Larry was really happy. He never claimed to be Donovan's grandfather, just acted like it, kind and happy toward Donovan and me. I'll always be thankful for Larry, and I'll always miss him."

I was aware throughout the meeting, but especially as Diane was speaking her heart for Larry, that Donovan was beaming, calm, self-contained, aware, serene. He was the quietest most fully present toddler I had ever seen at an A.A. meeting. Or maybe my imagination cast the image of loving grace on him, that substance which imperfect humans inherit from each other when there is respect, acceptance and friendship among them. I felt graced to look on Donovan at that moment.

at or to

Howard had not shown up the meeting yet. That had worried me (just as on the evening of Larry's death it had worried me that Keith and I for a long time could not find Howard). When he did finally walk into the meeting room I could see by his look he had considered not coming at all, had feared the emotion he might be exposed to or erupt with at Larry's posthumous A.A. birthday meeting. My smile back at Howard, my nod, were meant to convey to him that his coming was a moral victory which I understood and applauded.

Then I did speak. As briefly as I could before the whole group I told Howard why I thought of him as a hero, not for having tried to resuscitate Larry that recent Tuesday afternoon, but for having seen his friend so clearly and lovingly that morning as they ate breakfast and talked. I tried to tell Howard that the true friendship we are privileged to share in the Fellowship was succinctly and artistically displayed in that moment of true friendship which he had himself spontaneously done and remembered.

I probably spoke too long, said too many words to try to get my thought across, but so did the rest of us as we spoke one after the other for over an hour and a half. I felt self-conscious to have spoken at all when I had intended to stay silent so I could drink it all in, the reality of the Fellowship. I didn't feel too bad for too long, though, because everyone else seemed to have accepted what I said and how I said it, so I felt okay for me to accept me too.

Larry's children each spoke. Those were not the sorts of eulogies you might hear prepared for a public speech at a formal memorial, but rather straight personal testimony about what was present, recent and also long past. They recalled some pleasant but sketchy images of a father who laughed with them, played ball, went fishing.

They made clear a picture of the past each of us alcoholics is too painfully familiar with, that their father had been unreliable, unpredictable, disruptive and disappointing. Their mother and they had adapted to a life without him (no net loss at the time). They acknowledged he had later gradually come back into their lives peripherally, even in positive ways, especially this last Thanksgiving visit with them and their children.

What was news to them was the respect and love Larry had earned and enjoyed among his friends during the sixteen years since he had become sober. They had not seen their father as a respectable man, a citizen, a worker, an athlete, a friend. They had tended to carry a picture of him as a derelict, an invalid, a sick person who could give them little or nothing, who would more likely need their help. They thanked us for having given them the wholeness of their father.

Larry Junior turned to Diane to thank her especially, to accept her as a sister whom he had never known nor even heard of. Larry's children had begun to see and accept their father as a real man a while before he died, at Thanksgiving together with him and their own children. Now his value and his realness as a man and as a father had been confirmed again by everything said in this meeting, especially by Diane's words, by Donovan's presence.

Larry's children had brought the American flag which had covered Larry's casket. (He was a Navy veteran.) They regretted having taken his body away from Denver so quickly as they had, to bury him in the religious institution of his surviving sisters in Omaha. Now they considered he had had little regard for that particular church, and his sisters little regard for him, their black sheep brother. A few weeks earlier they had not known their father had a home and family to be laid to rest in, the Fellowship of Alcoholics Anonymous, the York Street Club.

We reassured them they had done right to rush his body back to Omaha. We didn't need his body for our memorial birthday meeting, since we carried his living person in our hearts. We welcomed them as family into our community.

They gave the carefully folded flag to Howard. There were hugs and birthday cake for everyone.

11

One Day at a Time

I really don't care much about putting myself into stories (the artist lurks in his work anyhow); but since these anecdotes are all so personal and from my heart, I guess I'll tell you about it. This is about the strength of friendship in the Fellowship not just at York Street but at every A.A. meeting place across the world. It's not just in A.A. (where we consciously and purposely nurture our humanness), but wherever and whenever people are willing to be of service to others, even today as I see in doctors and nurses and family and friends. It's all about persons I live with, some dead, some feline, but all very real.

As I was trying to finish these vignettes during the year that followed Larry's death, I suffered a severe heart attack. As an aftermath of the bypass surgery all my vital organs failed and I was unconscious, then delirious, about as hopeless as I have ever been. My wife, three years really and truly sober, was with me around the clock for a month. She called the Surgical Intensive Care Unit our honeymoon suite (since we had never really taken a honeymoon). I know it was hell for her.

I made it hell for the nurses, too, no doubt. Gracefully they took my curses and blows, my desperate driven attempts to escape from being cared for, my frantic foolish pullings-out and -off of my intravenous lines, oxygen mask and every other life-saving help. I furiously fought the restraints which saved me. I even pulled out my urinary catheter with my toes, balloon still inflated in my bladder. I made it hell for the nurses, and I regret it deeply now. I made it hell for the nurses, but when I came back to make amends, all they cared was that I was alive.

But the one who was in *real* hell was me. I remember it all, in my own way, and I knew immediately it was the same hell Big George had been through a mere year earlier. My son early on said, "Now Dad knows where the snack bar is in hell." Bingo! That reminded me of an episode before I got sober when he said, "Dad, when they start the Third World War, you'll take responsibility." (What a savvy ACOA![13])

In my delirium I was quite aware of my own agonizing conflicts. They may not make a lot of rational or worldly sense, but they were my own naked dying heart to me. Such things are not easily or gracefully expressed. It may also be difficult to see the egotism, the self-centeredness, the grandiosity in a pathologic altruist (which all clinicians are, and all "people-pleasers" and "co-dependents," I suppose).

My delirium had a center, guilt for the poor babies. I was convinced I had had to compromise the welfare of a child (my wife's youngest daughter, perhaps) because I was just not strong enough or smart enough to protect her from the world. I honestly (though deliriously) believed I was going through real hell, facing real death and real guilt, because I was not good enough to be an adequate (i.e., omnipotent) parent or physician.

My delirium had fringes, bizarre fantasies which went on day to day, distorting the "real" persons, places and things about me into a very different set which were of idiosyncratic significance. Besides the peanut people and the hidden sources of radiation, besides the underwater jet boats and the complex geography of the continent, besides the complex geometry of the building, I was sure I saw three cats at the screen door at the end of a long (nonexistent) hallway. I could just make them out as Samson and Calypso (who live with us now) and Butterscotch (who disappeared over twenty years ago).

As I slowly came alive my wife told me how close she and my two grown children had become while they spent day and night in the hospital during my delirium. My sister and my mother had come also. The five of them became real family over me while I was out of it, gone, not present.

I realized how close and supportive Angela's children and mine had been, and in the teary sentimental waning delirium I got resolution to my life-threatening moral dilemma: My unrealistic guilty responsibility for all children, all babies, was what had helped me be a dedicated and sensitive physician, even when I had been drunk; but the real children could take risks and make choices and take responsibility (as my own had done), and they could even take care of me. So, I was off the grandiosity hook if I were willing to be.

Being unconscious helped me gradually to become conscious. As well as a sense of the heart of my own internal conflicts, I had a distinct sense of every prayer said for me, every good thought or wish, and I could feel them sustain me. Even "bad" wishes helped, from the angry persons who had reason to cast thoughts my way, those I had somehow offended or alienated over the years; they were energy and they were for me.

I lay in a hospital bed right across the street from the one in which Jim had died exactly a year earlier. I became aware especially of the lesson he had given me in his second First Step: that sobriety is a way of living gracefully and in good humor, neither giving up nor taking over. Unconscious, I was developing a closer conscious contact with my higher power.

These few weeks since I have become conscious again have taught me a lot of the Program I had thought I had made progress with before. When I was fighting and cursing unconsciously, when gradually I became conscious and heard and watched myself doing that madness, I began to believe for the first time the label of "manic" the psychiatrists had sometimes given me.

After I came home, driven and determined to knock the world back into shape (for it had sagged sadly during my absence), I knew I would come to the end of me or of my madness, felt the change and crisis coming, had had too much experience with the Program not to know I was off base, in danger.

I called a friend in the Program, Jim M. He helped me see clearly that my fury was, of course, poorly camouflaged terror, and that all I could do with such fear was to "turn it over". I don't know how to turn it over any better than any of the rest of us, but I know it works, and I know how to be willing, and I know how to pray. That's enough, one day at a time.

While I was unconscious I was supposed to have helped Helen (Diane's mother, yes, that very ex-wife of Larry) and Jim M. get married at the Club. Helen had asked me to do the service on the landing of the front stairs, above D.P.R. I told her I couldn't do a wedding ceremony, that I am a doctor, not a preacher or a judge. She knew that; they would privately get married at the courthouse that morning, then I would do a public ceremony at the club that afternoon.

I had prepared a service, but couldn't deliver it to them until I had recovered from my surgery and could come home to print it out from my word processor[14]. Ironically, the judge they had gotten that morning at random was the one who had married Angela and me a few months earlier, my old friend in a hundred different dimensions. I called him to thank him for doing the job for me.

Helen and Jim were the first couple to have a wedding in the Club in a long time, but not the first mates in recovery together to marry. It seems just right to me that they had their wedding at the Club because I know their lives together are anchored in the A.A. Program. It is the same for Angela and me, and for Keith and Susan[15] and for a lot of others who have found new lives in the Program.

There is something which seems different between men and women in recovery, some different idiom of having suffered, some different style of having caused damage to others, some difference in the shape of shame and guilt. I think in general it is the woman whom society has trained to hide her guilt behind having been the victim (to deny having been the perpetrator). I suspect men hide shame behind the claim they still have strength, are somehow intact (denying they have suffered real personal injury, lest they cry aloud).

I hope we couples who come together in the maturity of our recoveries bring together a sense of peace between the man and the woman, the chance to be equals, perhaps, in shame and guilt, each of us having been tornadoes in the lives of others, and at the same time "our troubles, we believe, were of our own making." I hope we can become partners beyond all suffering and destruction. I hope we can become happy, joyous and free together.

Maturity in recovery is not a matter of years, of course, but of somehow coming to a way of real and full living through the Program. (Before, what I had was no way of life but a way of dying slowly and killing all the love around me.) Maturity in recovery seems not so much to be in the lessons which evoke "Ahas" as those daily relearnings better described by the duller phrase "Oh yeah." I look not so much for burning bushes today as for the confirmation of old principles in new insights.

Our Big Book doesn't say a lot out loud about maturity in sobriety. Clearly and for pressing reasons the text focuses on how hopeless our alcoholism had become and how to help one another get and stay sober. It vividly describes our past up to present but makes less concrete allusions toward the future ("more will be revealed"). I am beginning to understand that between the lines there are messages which shed some light on why I and many of my friends had given up the possibility of living with a partner (having failed so often by our own efforts in the past or having been deprived of the good we wished for by factors out of our control which seemed hostile toward us). We had become cynical about the institution of marriage and about any other major commitments to work, family or community.

It seems silly to me today to have had such a dramatic episode as heart attack, surgery, delirium, complications. Perhaps I have felt compelled be a man, always macho, always able, always right. If the purpose of it all was to come to an attitude of "Slow me down, Lord…" I had seen that all through my years in the Program. A mere month before my physical crisis I had written:

Thinking takes him time. Perhaps it is not thinking at all. He pauses at the small junctures with which his little life confronts him, pauses brief or long. Perhaps it is not something which occurs through time, but just another confrontation, another puzzle from which he cannot wish to draw his concentration. It is what is just before him; it is his little life.

Samson, the fat old cat, moves slowly, reacts mildly. He is a pussycat, not any way feral. He lives, has always lived, in a few rooms whose corners and furniture are never quite familiar. Any slightest change will stymie him, freeze him in his tracks; or if there is no change, no chair left in his way out from under the table, just the concrete presence of those elemental obstacles the walls themselves unmoving, they may give him cause to ponder, if this is pondering.

Although I have paid too little attention to his example, somehow just living with him has kept me alive for many years. By nature I am fast and far and in every direction, so no doubt I would have smashed me on the rocks long since, trying to fly through them. But some part of each day I am confronted by his plodding, a deep and simple wisdom unencumbered by intelligence. I do not emulate him, but somehow his simplicity moderates me just enough to save me.

He seems to feel no discomfort confronted by conundra, accepts them without judgement. It is not unlike my own inertia when I am for a time stuck on the shoals of my uncharted shores, depressed. I am often frozen, unable to move beyond obstacles I do not comprehend. But I do not have the wisdom to contemplate them out of time; I rush to fight them within me, flagellate myself for not soaring past them, ruminate and judge and figure futilely.

I have the opportunity today to emulate this pussycat, relinquish all considerations, to live only in the little world at the end of my nose. A million times I have had the opportunity to be serene, disdained it; but today, this morning, this little moment out of time, perhaps…

12-06-96

I'm a bit calmer, a bit slower and a bit more well than a week ago, a month ago. God willing, I will live for the duration with the beautiful people who are my family and my Fellowship. I can't tell you how good it is to be alive, relearning the same old lessons each day. I still rely on ghosts to guide me, especially Butterscotch. Maybe you will meet him on the road…

12

My Final Chapter at York Street

Today I am alive in many mundane and imperfect ways: I have challenging employment, a stable marriage, grown children who are struggling in the world, extended family with ordinary problems including life-threatening ones. I have several friends, most of them in the Fellowship of Alcoholics Anonymous. My health and energy are diminishing, but mercifully slowly.

This is not my last chapter because I am myself dying at the moment, nor am I about to relapse drinking nor any other form of suicide. But this morning I end my relationship with the York Street Club as it has been for fifteen years. I no longer can center my life and growth exactly here at this old house spatially, temporally or socially. This is not where I will invest my energy, although I pray God continue to reposit plenty of Her power here.

In the previous chapters of this book, developed from the moment I walked up these steps, I have tried to give you a taste of what works, what can be good about an A.A. club or group or meeting-place. Spiritually these can never disappear, only keep growing. But I told you at the beginning[16] that York Street has a long history of chaos and instability, and for some of us there may come a time, as for me today, when we must let go arrogant pretensions in the guise of altruism.

I may stay around, but I won't again try to run the place, not even if it seems to be slipping down the drain again. I will do as I have watched others do, as Bill Wilson has described in the "Twelve and Twelve" and elsewhere—avoid becoming a "bleeding deacon" who insists on imposing his will onto those around him even if it kills him.

I thank God I usually have not slipped into that mentality, but I sure see the dangers. Of course I see it acted out by others—that's always easy to see. I don't want to look back over my shoulder and see it having been acted out by me. (I recall early in sobriety looking back over my shoulder, gasping in horror, tearfully wailing to see the six-year-old at a Bar Mitzvah getting drunk on sweet sacramental wine, not drunk enough yet, spinning in circles to make himself dizzy on top of it.)

It is something with which we are quite familiar on at least two levels: that through the tools of the Program we come gradually to see the faults in ourselves we previously had thoroughly been blind to (the compulsion to drink, the compulsion to control, the compulsion to be admired); and the inexorable certainty that after we have examined and acknowledged our weaknesses once, we will encounter the very same in ourselves again any number of times in various disguises until, perhaps, only by the grace of God, someday they may have diminished.

These tools of the Program are condensed in the words of the Fourth and Tenth Steps as, "Made a fearless and thorough moral inventory of ourselves," and "Continued to take personal inventory and when we were wrong promptly admitted it."

Personal recovery and sobriety seem easy to maintain once we have really got started at being honest, as long as we have others who really know how to use these tools, who really understand. In many A.A. meeting groups we have watched individuals continuing successfully to help other individuals. When someone can't quite get started, or when someone relapses, we attribute that to the stubborn destructiveness of the Disease.

When new meeting groups get started we see it as growth of the Fellowship and of the Program. Often a new group has splintered from an old group because of some conflict between individuals, but the conflict appears to be resolved (or at least decompressed) by the separation, so the Program and the Fellowship still look powerful.

Sometimes we watch meeting groups dwindle and die, but their individual members can always go to other groups or start new ones, so the pain is ameliorated by the appearance of continuity of support for each individual who has a desire to stay sober.

In <u>A.A. Comes of Age</u>[17] Bill Wilson describes in some detail the survival of A.A. through some of its earlier phases, through conflict between individuals, between groups, between regions. He makes it clear to me how the Twelve Traditions of the group and the Twelve Concepts of service were developed to stabilize this project beyond the personalities of the Founders, how he and Bob worked long and hard with all the rest of us to allow them to set aside the reins.

A.A.'s Traditions and Concepts seem to have helped the organization as a whole (not without difficulty) to survive and grow, but those principles have not been used effectively at York Street. Some other place and time I am willing help you chronicle the recurrent tidal waves of disparate egos which have torn at the vessel of this Club (a Club inventory, if you will), but for today let it suffice for me to report as Secretary of the Board the minutes of the recent meeting (February 20, 2003):

> **Present:** All seven Board members (Chris M., chair), the Manager, the Accountant and upwards of two dozen persons, most of whom are probably dues-paying members (though no count was taken).
>
> **Call to order:** About 5:34 P.M., with the Serenity Prayer.
>
> **Minutes:** The minutes of the previous meetings, January 22 and January 29 were read and accepted by the Board.
>
> **Business:** The Chairperson began to introduce an issue involving the suspension from the Club by the Manager

of two Board members and another Club member (Gary Mc., Dave N. and Scott R.) for arguments and altercations the previous week. Somehow it was thereupon decided to rescind the suspensions. Before any call for reports or business in order, Board member Bill W. moved, and it was seconded by Dave N., (in concert with a background chorus throughout the room of complaints about the Board's previous meeting and action) that the previous meeting be acknowledged as illegal and that the Board offer a written apology to the members. No clear vote of the Board on this motion was reached, although a piece of paper was passed for signature (the entirety of the text, "Members we apologize"). The ensuing discussion, though not controlled by the Chairperson nor apparently in any way orderly, was fairly clear in its development and conclusion. In brief: that the By-laws (5.107) state that Board meetings shall at all times be open to members, but the selection of a Manager on January 29 was done in a closed session. It was clarified by Nathan P. that matters of confidentiality in personnel determinations and similar legally sensitive considerations had throughout the previous years (during which he had himself served on the Board three separate times) been held in confidence. Carroll G., agreeing some matters should be accomplished in executive session, articulately accused Nathan (with the opprobrium, "Shame on you!") of having himself formulated those By-laws (in 1992) and now ignoring them (to which Nathan countered that the By-laws appropriately might have been revised long since had Carroll himself not consistently obstructed such action in membership meetings over the previous year). Dennis C., citing extensive experience with various boards, suggested that although the interviews and considerations might well be shared in confidential Board session, the decision itself should be made in a properly open Board meeting. Further complaints regarding the behavior of the Board in relation to the By-laws included the lack of prior posting of agendas for Board meetings (to be prepared by the Chairperson, posted three days prior to the meeting, 5.108). Further discussion acknowledging the instability over the past several months of the Club's administration (six Managers, three Board Chairpersons, five separate regimes in the Café, et cetera) seemed to have no effect on the persistent tenor that the Board had not followed the By-laws. The Chairperson summarized that the previous discussion made clear the need to adjourn the present meeting, to set a new meeting date the next week for which all proper postings could be prepared, confirmed there was no further business at the moment, stated his resignation from the Board (but politely stayed for the closing of the meeting). Subsequently it was clarified by several present referring to the By-laws that (5.201), "The Board of Directors may by majority vote select and employ a Club Manager," without specification of what sort of session (open or closed) may be required. The remaining Board members chose Dave N. to preside at the next session.

Adjournment: 6:17 P.M. with the Lord's Prayer.

Respectfully submitted,
Nathan P., Secretary to the Board

So, you can see that it seems to me we as a community in recovery are quite imperfectly able to carry on our business. What is our business? It can hardly be other than to pursue A.A.'s primary purpose, to carry the message to all alcoholics and to practice the principles in all our affairs (Twelfth Step).

Some say clubs are not A.A., just associated businesses renting space for meetings, selling coffee or burgers or books. The General Services Office (what you might call A.A. world headquarters) hardly acknowledges clubs exist; their pyramidal concept consists of individuals, groups, regions, districts, et cetera.

But if the Steps, the Traditions and the Concepts are the tools which allow those units to function without self-destructing, the same tools likely will be useful for clubs. Perhaps some clubs use them well, but not York Street in the beginning (fifty-five years ago when it came about as a rancorous split of Denver's A.A. community), not the past fifteen years I have been here, and especially not the last six months or so.

The Sixth Tradition was formulated about the time York Street got started, for us and for other communities suffering some of those earlier internal conflicts. It advises that "An

A.A. group ought never endorse, finance, or lend the A.A. name to any related facility or outside enterprise, lest problems of money, property, and prestige divert us from our primary purpose."

It doesn't much matter whether I or the majority of us at York Street intend to stay sober and to help other alcoholics to achieve sobriety, if as a community we constantly engage in decisions based on self. The First Tradition is difficult for us to live: Our common welfare should come first; personal recovery depends on A.A. unity. It doesn't matter how well-motivated we conceive ourselves if we are repeatedly riven by conflicts of money, property, prestige and their petty concomitants pride, greed, lust, anger, gluttony, envy, and sloth.

An amazing and revolutionary concept arose early on in A.A.—group conscience. Bill Wilson illustrates it in the "Twelve and Twelve" in his discussion of the Second Tradition: For our group purpose there is but one ultimate authority—a loving God as He may express Himself in our group conscience. Our leaders are but trusted servants; they do not govern.

In our Western self-centered culture we have institutions based on authority, self-interest, entitlement, enfranchisement, property rights, lobbying, adversarial rights, representation, majority rule—these are quite the opposite of group conscience. When the simple group conscience principle is used it pivots not on answers but on questions, not on voting but on consensus, not on closure (coming to the bottom line) but on openness, not on division but on sharing.

I like to use the rule of thumb that instead of coming together in the same room each armed with our brilliant ideas, we instead come with empty minds, openness to God's will for us. This means trusting God and each other. It has been difficult to come to at York Street probably, as many say, because we are a group of very sick persons. But our sickness has brought us to discover and to use powerful new tools like group conscience, service to others, principles before personalities—anodynes to the destructive egotism our disease imposed on ourselves and everyone about us.

The only thing I know to do now is to disengage my own ego from the fray. I may come to meetings here, I may share coffee with my friends at York Street. I must continue to be available to the newcomer or any other alcoholic who still suffers (and we all still suffer). But I must not risk contributing to the insanity of a community so desperately in need of serenity, so I finish my book about friendship in the Fellowship by resigning from the Board. Let someone else write personal and group histories from now on, while I live my life. Next Thursday while the York Street Board is meeting an old teacher of mine is lecturing in Boulder, so I think I'll go to see him.

Endnotes

[1] The first "club" was in New York City. Older meeting groups and clubs are found in other places, but 1311 York Street is one of the longest in one place to the present. York Street was the one of the first clubs purchased by an A.A. group, and later had to be changed to a non-profit private social club, separate from the A.A. groups themselves. The Club in turn rents out meeting space to autonomous groups. Traditions Six and Seven were directed to the problems of money, property and authority which can surely destroy our spiritual heritage. Since there is no competition or prestige involved between the various clubs, only recovery and service, it matters little enough which is the oldest club. My stints on the board at York Street convinced me we could well enough afford to sell the building and rent a store-front on Colfax Avenue; A.A. would be the same program.

My friend John M. has written this note about the beginning of York Street, highlighting the irony that Larry McC's father organized opposition to it when Larry was a kid, only to be thankful later that Larry sobered up here. Larry is still sober and still hangs around York Street volunteering service regularly.

> To Denver, in 1948, A.A. was a relative newcomer, not at all well understood but sure as hell not enthusiastically welcomed anywhere. The generally held conception of A.A. was one of street bums and vagrants, derelicts and panhandlers plus a few retired ladies of the night getting together for God only knows what suspect purpose. The days of A.A. meetings held in the basements of Protestant churches or in a neighborhood store-front were still a time down the road. Few persons had even heard of A.A. and those that had weren't particularly interested in expanding their acquaintance. Having an A.A. meeting hall for a next door neighbor was a conception then about as remote as a moon landing.

> Capitol Hill in 1948 was an upscale affluent neighborhood, one of Denver's finest, to be sure. Let us simplify the subject by saying that the idea of having an A.A. meeting hall in their midst hadn't even crossed the minds of the locals.

Members of Denver's original A.A. group, *Group One*, had been meeting in a second floor walk-up near 16th and Broadway in downtown Denver since 1945. Some well-acquainted members of Group One had learned that a property at 1311 York Street was in a bit of financial distress. The building might make an ideal central meeting facility for Group One. It was on the sale block. The Group was well aware that A.A. might not be too welcome in the heart of Capitol Hill even though some of the members of the recently formed group were also numbered among the affluent Capitol Hill residents. When it came to procuring the York Street property, so totally suitable as a city-wide A.A. center, the Group One members moved swiftly and silently. Financing was put in place, contracts were signed <u>and the deal was closed</u>, all before most of the Capitol Hill neighborhood even knew that A.A. existed, let alone what had happened in their neighborhood. Clever chaps, those drunks.

But then the "stuff" hit the fan. A Cheesman Park neighbor and well known activist, Jim R. McC. rose up in righteous wrath. McC. lived at 1259 Columbine Street, just across 13th Avenue from 1311 York Street. McC. solicited the neighborhood in an effort to stem this invasion of his homeland by a drunken horde. Meetings were held, speeches were made, petitions were circulated and signed. Everything short of a vigilante mob was considered.

Alas, all to no avail. Group One's founding fathers had been quick and thorough, and their deal was done. Denver A.A. had a new home at 1311 York Street. There were quiet rumors of some covert support of A.A.'s property acquisition from a few local influential politicos. Even then it was a well known but well camouflaged fact that several of the local big shots could well have used more than a little A.A. help. But, be that as it may...

Jim McC. and the neighbors were left to lick their wounded prides and fear the worst. However, as relates to this writer and a lot of other drunks, all of this activity was indeed good, for it soon came to pass that none other than Jim McC's eldest son Larry was to become one of my early A.A. sponsors. I originally met Larry McC at 1311 York Street in 1969. He had about three years of sobriety at the time. So, now you know "the rest of the story."

[2] Various descriptions of the earlier history of the building and its occupants are found in histories of Denver, a recent popular specimen of which is

<u>Ghosts of Denver: Capitol Hill</u> by Phil Goodstein, New Social Publications, Denver, 1996. Unfortunately, they are probably all wrong. Annie A., one of our members, has produced a more accurate history now. She has checked archival sources and has even interviewed a granddaughter of the former owner, who recalls growing up here.

1311 YORK STREET, DENVER:
A HISTORY OF OUR "MOTHER HOUSE"
by Annie A.

BEGINNINGS
HOME TO JUDGE LEFEVRE
HISTORY OF TWO BENEFACTORS
THE TRANSITION TO ALCOHOLICS
ANONYMOUS

> *"Many a man, yet dazed from his hospital experience has stepped over the threshold of that home into freedom. Many an alcoholic who entered there came away with an answer. He succumbed to that gay crowd inside, who laughed at their own misfortunes and understood his. Impressed by those who visited him at the hospital, he capitulated entirely when, later, in an upper room of this house, he heard the story of some man whose experience closely tallied with his own. The expression on the faces of the women, that indefinable something in the eyes of the men, the stimulating and electric atmosphere of the place, conspired to let him know that here was haven at last."*
>
> —(about the Williams house in Akron
> from "A Vision for You,"
> Chapter 11 of the Big Book,
> <u>Alcoholics Anonymous</u>,
> page 160)

BEGINNINGS

An unimportant item in "The Western Architect and Building News", in March, 1891 read: "A $10,000 residence is being erected at Thirteen Ave-

nue and York Street, for Charles Taylor, of the firm of Taylor & Rathyon"
(The Western Architect and Building News, March, 1891. Vol. 11, No. 13,
p. 198). Little could anyone guess the significance of that notice for the future
of early Alcoholics Anonymous in Denver.

Who was Charles Taylor? He came to Colorado in 1879 and located at Red
Cliff, Eagle County to pursue his interests in mining as a financier and mining manager. He was vigilant about seeking prospect properties out of which
mines could be made by developmental work, and was not afraid to take hold
of anything he felt would have merit, even contrary to popular opinion. He
had faith in mineral veins and was confident in his judgment of them, believing a claim should be worked vigorously to decide whether or not it was valu-
able. His executive faculties were brilliant and he had great personal charisma.
The firm of Taylor & Rathyon were successful in placing stocks of various
mines controlled by them and were able to induce investors to put $350,000
into mining properties just on their personal representation.

Charles Taylor owned the property and built the house at 1311 York Street,
purchased by Judge Owen LeFevre in the early 1900's. Judge Owen LeFevre,
judge of the District Court of Denver, was a native of Ohio. He was born
August 6, 1848, in the village of Little York, Montgomery county, of that
state. From the district school in Little York and the grade schools of Dayton,
he entered Antioch College. In 1868 he entered the University of Michigan
and in 1872 was admitted to practice by the Supreme Court of Ohio. He
entered the law office of John A. McMahon and George W. Houck, two
noted Ohio lawyers at Dayton, and remained with them until the summer of
1873, when he came to Denver to practice law. Judge LeFevre established a
home in the suburban town of Highlands. In 1875 he was elected attorney
for Highlands and was re-elected in 1876. In 1885 he was chosen its Mayor
and was re-elected. He was next called as attorney for Arapahoe county by the
County Commissioners, and was re-elected to this position. In 1892 he was
elected judge of the County Court, on the Republican ticket. In 1894 he was
elected one of the Judges of the Second Judicial District for Arapahoe
County. Upon his retirement from the District bench in January, 1901, he
resumed private practice. (Smiley, Jerome C., History of Denver, The Denver Times, The Times-Sun Publishing Company, Denver, 1901, pages 574,
651, 696, 697, 714, as well as interview with Mrs. Frederica Lincoln.)

HOME TO JUDGE LEFEVRE

Owen LeFevre married Eva French of Troy, Ohio, June 28, 1871. They had one daughter, Frederica. They resided in Highlands until 1896 when they occupied their home at 1311 York street. "It is adorned with what is perhaps the most choice collection of modern French paintings in Colorado, and is a center of art, literature, and music. Judge LeFevre is a lover of books, and his home library, in which by all standards, is one of the best in the city of Denver" (Ibid). Judge LeFevre died in 1921. The LeFevres' one child, Frederica, became the wife of Harry Bellamy, a partner in a Denver stationary store and printing company Kendrick-Bellamy. Harry Bellamy was born in 1874, and died in 1956. Frederica Bellamy died in 1963. The Bellamys lived from about 1915 at 1174 Race street, built about 1900, where she lived until her death. The Bellamys' daughter, Frederica married Colonel George Arthur Lincoln. "Colonel Lincoln was well-known for his service to the country: aide to General Marshall in WWII, Head of the Department of Social Sciences at West Point, many times military and political advisor, and among many other accomplishments, was in charge of the Office of Emergency Preparedness." (Smiley, Jerome C., History of Denver, The Denver Times, The Times-Sun Publishing Company, Denver, 1901.)

"After the death of Mrs. Owen J. LeFevre on June 13, 1948 she was reported to have left an estate valued in excess of $115,000, as shown in her will filed for probate in County Court disclosed. A daughter, Eva F. Bellamy, 1174 Race St., would receive a large portion of her mother's estate. Under terms of the will she would receive 150 shares of preferred stock of the U.S. Steel Corp., several parcels of real estate and jewelry. Mrs. Bellamy's husband, Harry, was left several lots of real estate. A granddaughter, Frederica Lincoln, West Point, N.Y., was given 300 shares of preferred stock in the U.S. Steel Corp. Sums ranging from $300 to $500 were left to several religious and philanthropic institutions and organizations" (Rocky Mountain News, 6-30-48).

"To Mrs. Owen E. LeFevre, for things she has done to advance its progress, to add to the beauty and goodness, to promote the welfare of the helpless and needy, to make religion a living thing, Denver and its people of all ranks owe congratulations and good wishes for 'many happy returns of the day' on this, the ninetieth anniversary of her birth" (Denver Post, 10-20-41)

HISTORY OF TWO BENEFACTORS

Both Mrs. Bellamy and Mrs. Lincoln came by their philanthropic efforts from the preceding work of their mother and grandmother, Eva LeFevre. It is essential to devote a brief history of these two women, because it is through their generosity and ultimate decisions that 1311 York Street became entrusted to Alcoholics Anonymous.

EVA FREDERICA LEFEVRE BELLAMY

"Mrs. Bellamy was born Eva Frederica LeFevre on January 6, 1884 in Denver to Eva and Owen LeFevre. She attended Wolcott School in Denver and Bryn Mawr College and studied singing in Germany, Italy and France. Shortly after she returned home she was a member of seven charity agency boards and she's never been inactive since. She sang soprano for organizations and local opera and was soloist for several years at Central Presbyterian Church. A horsewoman then, she showed thoroughbreds in a number of shows. At that time she lived at 1400 Josephine Street. The Bellamys have one daughter, named Frederica after her mother. She was married to Col. George Arthur Lincoln, an assistant professor at West Point, and then was serving at the Pentagon". (Rocky Mountain News, 4-22-51). "Among her avocations she was a lecturer, writer and producer of religious drama,. as well as newspaper work. She was also a book reviewer as well as a foreign correspondent." (Portrait Collection of Denver Public Library) "She has been associated with most of the civic activities in Denver…She was head of the Denver Blood Bank of the American Red Cross and an organizer of the women's guild of the Denver Symphony Orchestra (Rocky Mountain News, 5-13-45).

FREDERICA BELLAMY LINCOLN

"Freddie" Bellamy Lincoln was born on May 9, 1915 in Denver to Harry and Frederica LeFevre Bellamy. "I resided at 1174 Race Court, four blocks from my grandparents' (the LeFevre's) home. At an early age I often walked to Granny's house. As her only grandchild I often stayed with her and it was a second home to me. I particularly loved the third floor with all the books and the balcony. I attended Wolcott School and then Kent School where I graduated in 1932. I graduated from Bryn Mawr College in 1936 with honors in history of art. This interest was perhaps inspired by the paintings in the LeFevre house and my own.

"Lieutenant George Arthur Lincoln and I were married in 1936 in St. John's Cathedral and our wedding reception was held at 1311 York Street. As an Army wife, I resided first in Huntington, West Virginia and then at West Point, New York, where my husband was an instructor at the United States Military Academy. I returned to Denver with two children when Captain Lincoln was overseas in World War II. Our household belongings were stored in the basement of 1311 York Street. My husband was ordered to Washington, D.C., and we lived there until 1947. He served as Professor of Social Sciences. Our family of four children grew up at West Point. My husband retired as Brigadier General and we moved to Washington, D.C., where he headed the Office of Emergency Preparedness. In 1973 we came to Evergreen, Colorado where I now reside.

"I was a volunteer nurse's aide under a Red Cross program from 1943 to 1953, serving in two hospitals in the Washington area and the in the West Point Hospital. I was a Girl Scout leader for several years and on the Board of the Army Relief Society (now defunct). I volunteered in two elementary schools in Washington. Currently I am active in the local Jefferson County Historical Society, the American Association of University Women, and the Evergreen Animal Protective League. In Denver I am on the committee for College for a Day, and I am a member of the Monday Literary Society (as was my grandmother).

"I have been fortunate to have traveled extensively in Europe, Latin America, the Middle East, the Far East, and Africa. I rode and showed horses in my youth and since returning to Colorado I can enjoy several horses in my backyard. I have dabbled in the arts, first singing, painting much later, copper enameling and, for the last six years, writing poetry.

"My husband died in 1975 and our youngest daughter, Lorna, in 1981. Our other three children, Frederica Riahi, Daniel Lincoln and Joyce Conrey, all live in this area with their spouses, to my great joy. I have four grandchildren: Elizabeth Stieren, Curtis Lincoln, Douglas and Frederica Conrey. There are three great grandchildren: Sean and Lorna Stieren and Grayson Lincoln."

TRANSITION TO ALCOHOLICS ANONYMOUS

After her mother's death, Mrs. Bellamy called her daughter, Freddie Lincoln in West Point, New York to discuss what should be done with the property at

1311 York street. Mrs. Bellamy explained to Freddie that there had been several offers made with regard to sale of the property. A chiropractor (Dr. Speer) who claimed to cure cancer was anxious to buy the property, but Mrs. Bellamy felt this man may not have been entirely credible and she did not wish to support sale of the property to him. Then, there was the suggestion by the City to make the property into a rooming house. This was not acceptable to Mrs. Bellamy either. A dentist also wanted to purchase the property in order to remodel it into a suite of offices. Mrs. Bellamy declined this offer. Mrs. Bellamy was looking for a humanitarian approach to the sale of the property, which would serve and enhance the community. Alcoholics Anonymous had approached her regarding the sale of the property at 1311 York Street. Both Mrs. Bellamy and Mrs. Lincoln agreed enthusiastically that this would be the most humanitarian effort to serve a need in the community (Interview with Mrs. Frederica Lincoln, 4-30-98 at her Evergreen, Colorado home).

Dissatisfaction with the facilities at 1608 Broadway surfaced in steering committee meetings as early as 1947 (Denver Post, 1-15-49). In August of 1947 members discussed appointing a building committee to contact realtors and individuals with regard to finding better facilities. A special meeting was held a week later and the tone was discouraging. The price of real estate was too high for the Committee to consider purchasing property for a club at the time. A temporary solution to the problem of space was sought in renting the auditorium of the Tramway Building in downtown Denver. By June of 1948 it was clear the idea of using the Tramway Building was a failure. The building was too hard to find, and the impersonal atmosphere of the place was all wrong for A.A. meetings (1990 Colorado Area Archives Committee, History of Colorado A.A., p. 36). For this reason in July of 1948 a new building committee spearheaded by Jim H. was named to chair a Building Committee to search the city for a larger building. (1990 Colorado Area Archives Committee, History of Colorado A.A. p. 36). Six weeks later a building finance committee headed by Don B. was assigned the same task (1990 Colorado Area Archives Committee, History of Colorado A.A. p. 36). Shortly thereafter this committee came up with a building for consideration at 2501 Woodbury Court which the committee felt might be suitable for group #1 and could be purchased for a reasonable cost. The owner wanted $1750 for option to purchase. Several members of the steering committee agreed to look at the structure. Concerns that the location at 2501 Woodbury Court might be purchased without sufficient consideration from Group #1 arose. It was suggested that members of Group #1 familiar with real estate prices and construction work inspect the Woodbury Court Building. As a result a new building committee was formed and charged with the responsibility of locating other sites and making recommendations to the steering committee, which apparently gave no further consideration to the building at 2501 Woodbury Court. The new committee was urged to work fast as conditions at 1608 Broadway were becoming more congested every week (1990 Colorado Area Archives Committee, History of Colorado A.A. p. 36-40). By December 14, 1948, less than three weeks after it's first meeting the committee had its first recommendation. The LeFevre estate, located at 1311 York street was for sale and could be had for $30,000. It was a spacious home, adequate to accommodate a club, headquarters, auditorium, and smaller meeting rooms.

On December 31, 1948, an article appeared in the Denver Post: "Juvenile Court Judge Philip B. Gilliam notified officials of Alcoholics Anonymous he supports a plan calling for public donations so the organization can purchase for $25,000 the home of the late Mrs. Owen LeFevre at 1311 York Street. Earlier District Judge Joseph E. Cook announced support. The home would be used for meetings, social gatherings, and for initial treatment of new members seeking a cure for alcoholism" (The Denver Post, Friday, Dec. 31, 1948)

On January 15, 1949, an article appeared in the Denver Post stating: "More than $6,000 has been donated in ten days by members of Alcoholics Anonymous toward purchase of a new home and meeting place at 1311 York Street, officials announced Saturday. The organization previously had been given ten days to collect $5,000 for a down payment on the old Owen LeFevre home at the York Street address, but donations soared over the collection goal. In publicizing the fund-raising drive, group officials pointed out that Denver is the only major city in the country in which Alcoholics Anonymous does not own its own meeting place. For five years the organization has had headquarters at 1608 Broadway. But swelling membership has forced officials to look elsewhere for a meeting place. Approximately 800 persons belong to the organization now, officials said. The LeFevre home will be remodeled into meeting quarters, recreational rooms and other facilities available to members." (The Denver Post, 1-15-49).

As late as April 10, 1949, the organization of Alcoholics Anonymous was still in the transition stage from 1608 Broadway to 1311 York Street. An excerpt from a Denver Post article reads: "A man drifts away from the central group, but he hasn't quit A.A. He's gone out and set up his own neighborhood group, of eight or ten or twelve persons. There might be up to twenty such groups in Denver right now, as anonymous as their name, paying dues to no one, nor communicating as a body with the national A.A., or the downtown group at 1608 Broadway, which soon will move to clubrooms recently bought at 1311 York." (The Denver Post, Sunday, April 10, 1949).

1311 York Street has been the landmark of Alcoholics Anonymous in Denver for the past fifty years.

[3] Myths convey the truth, whether or not they are exactly factual. I like the myth that the Sixth and Seventh Traditions (to be self-supporting, to avoid conflicts over power and money) got much of their impetus from the conflict in the Denver A.A. community over whether to own property, specifically this very house. When Bill visited in 1949 both factions looked to him to resolve the conflict. Bill is said to have said, "Well, it worked, didn't it? But I'd hate to see us try that again." I prefer to believe Bill simply said, "It's been nice seeing you fellas. I'm off to Los Angeles now."

[4] Especially Alcoholics Anonymous (the "Big Book") and The Twelve Steps and the Twelve Traditions (the "Twelve by Twelve"), available at any A.A. meeting-place or through Alcoholics Anonymous World Services, Inc., Box 459, Grand Central Station, New York, New York 10163.

[5] Especially in Pass It On and Doctor Bob and the Good Oldtimers, available at the same sources.

[6] Don Marquis, Archy and Mehitabel, Doubleday, 1927.

Kenneth Grahame, The Wind in the Willows, Methuen, 1908.

[7] "Dead Pecker Row" is the chair-lined wall of the central hallway at 1311 York Street where thousands have sat between meetings "shaking it out," afraid to walk onto the surrounding streets where there are bars and liquor stores.

[8] The morning I sat to write about George he was headed for surgery again, as I summarize later in the story. George subsequently died sober.

[9] But since I wrote this story God gave me a new car, and I gave the old one to Keith. The convolutions are too tedious, so if you are curious as to the details just ask me about it some time.

[10] Carl has completed his sentence in prison and a halfway house, has worked and grown, changed jobs from hospital records clerk to selling toe-rings, is sober and attending meetings in Hawaii.

[11] And life goes on. Every time I see the pattern of God's will it is clear to me, and the next moment or the next day God's will shifts to dimensions I never imagined. Keith remarried, Carl got out of prison, Matthew relapsed and sobered up again, but the program and the fellowship remain the simple same, always big enough for all of us.

[12] Called "the million dollar table" because of the millions that have been lost by those who sit there to drink coffee. Keith told me he had an intuition he would be a millionaire, and by the time he added up the debts on the house, the business and Anita's hospital bills before she died, he figured that came to close to a million, and he and the dogs were still eating. I guess anyone who can still eat and owes a million dollars is very like a millionaire.

[13] Adult Child of an Alcoholic.

[14] Here is the mush I had written before my heart attack:

For the Marriage of Jim and Helen M____
1311 York Street, Denver, Colorado
February 7, 1997

We are here in the spiritual ancestral home of our family, our community of recovery. We each came home to this familiar warmth from the same cold confusing wilderness. We have known loneliness as few do, even in a crowd, even in what seemed to be a family. So the newcomer here is as much an intimate part of this family as the crustiest long-timer.

Helen, Jim, we are all familiar with each other, all at home here. I do not have to welcome anyone nor officiate in any formal manner. All I have to do is to be brave enough to speak aloud what all here know, that the two of you will spend a rich life together one day at a time, and the more you spend the richer you will be.

Today we share no grandiose promises of a perfect future, just promises that we can be present with each other one day at a time. It is not merely enough, but a richness beyond what we could ourselves plan and choose. We have access to real love and real community, and we don't even secretly wish for anything unreal.

We could be skeptical about the institution of marriage, or at least about wedding ceremonies. We are experts at cynicism, criticism and prognostication (so we make bets on anything). But we know by experience not to judge ourselves or our friends in real life. The two of you propose to pool your imperfections. It is our privilege as your friends, your family, to support you and to cheer you on.

I hope these brief lines will be helpful for you:

> Love is not a gift,
> a grace, the saving
> of one's self from isolation.
> It is hard to say what love is,
> but that it is real,
> within reach.
> Love is immensely powerful,
> but not manipulable;
> you cannot *make* it work.
> Love comes
> only through willingness
> to be who I am
> without *thinking*
> of who I am
> or how I choose to be.
> Love comes
> only through willingness
> that you be
> who you are
> especially
> because I love you.
> Love is between us,
> not in you

or in me.
Because I live I love you,
give up all pretense
of choosing or controlling.
Because I live I trust you,
open my mouth
and close my eyes,
take what life gives me
to taste and share with you
freely together.
We need no guarantee,
nor need we be perfect
in our promises.
We need not fear
growing apart
if we grow together.
If love between us is
openness and willingness,
we lose nothing—
flowing into one another,
touching, being touched—
but gain us each forever.

I am lucky; there is no power granted to me except to be a friend. With all the power of my friendship I join you as you join each other. That is all I have to say, but we all know I can't keep anyone else from speaking her mind.

God bless you both with health and joy.

[15] Susan is Keith's new wife, who works with Helen, who just started the program, whom Keith first met at Helen and Jim M.'s wedding; they married each other the day before I am rewriting this paragraph. Real life is too intricate to be made into a soap opera.

[16] "The old house is solid enough but the Club is always shaky—too little money, too few members to support the old red white elephant. Decade by decade, debacle by debacle, the Club persists, not so much by any one's heroic efforts to save it, but (for all I know) by the will of God. Whenever

anyone tries to raise much money or to refurbish the innately elegant house, to upgrade wiring or to lay new carpet, it all evaporates in the egotism of those would-be heroes. So, money has been wasted or otherwise disappears, then things clunk along again much as they had been, despite all egotistic and altruistic efforts (and debt to Mister R's bank). Management frequently changes faces, but always scuttles, fudges and begs to make employment tax payments, utility bills, keep the Café open, patch the roof—all just to sustain the primary purpose, to keep the doors open for the next sick newcomer." Chapter 1, 2nd paragraph

[17] Alcoholics Anonymous Comes of Age, a Brief History of A.A., Alcoholics Anonymous World Services, New York 1957.

A Prayer
(adapted from the **"Big Book"**
and **The Twelve Steps and
the Twelve Traditions,**
in the order of the Steps)

God, grant me the serenity
to accept the ones I cannot change,
courage to change the *one* I can,
and wisdom to know the difference. (Steps I & II)
God, I offer my self to You
to build with me and do with me as You will.
Relieve me of the bondage of self
that I may better know and do Your will.
Take away my difficulties
that victory over them may bear witness
to those I would help
of Your power, Your love and Your way of life.
May I do Your will all ways. (III)
When others hurt me,
save me from being angry.
Save me from the need to be right or righteous.
Remove my fears.
Mold my ideals and help me live up to them.
Grant me sanity, tolerance,
patience, pity and good will
in relation to others.
Guide me to be helpful to them,

willing to make amends
where I have done harm. (IV)
I thank You from the bottom of my heart
for letting me know You and me better. (V)
Help me be willing to be who I am.
Help me be willing to love You
and to love my fellows.
Help me be willing
to love and to care for my self. (VI)
My Creator, I am now willing
that You should have all of me,
good and bad.
I pray You now take from me
every single defect of character
which stands in the way of my usefulness
to You and my fellows.
Grant me strength as I go out from here
to do Your bidding. (VII)
I pray for the willingness until it comes. (VIII)
Show me the way
of patience, tolerance, kindliness and love.
Let me know a new freedom
and a new happiness.
Free me from regret of the past.
Let me comprehend the word serenity
and let me know peace.

I pray my experience can benefit others.
Please, let my self-seeking slip away.
Take away my fears
so I can intuitively know
that You are doing for me
what I could not do for myself. (IX)
How can I best serve You?
Your will, not mine, be done. (X)
Forgive me.
Direct my thinking.
Give me an inspiration,
an intuitive idea, a decision.
Throughout the day show me
what my next step is to be,
the right thought, the right action. (XI)
Lord, make me a channel of Your peace—
that where there is hatred
I may bring love,
that where there is wrong
I may bring the spirit of forgiveness,
that where there is discord
I may bring harmony,
that where there is error
I may bring truth,
that where there is doubt
I may bring faith,

that where there is despair
I may bring hope,
that where there are shadows
I may bring light,
that where there is sadness
I may bring joy.
Lord, grant that I may seek
rather to comfort than to be comforted,
to understand than to be understood,
to love than to be loved—
for it is by forgetting that I may find,
by forgiving that I may be forgiven,
by being willing to face death
that I may awaken to true life. (XII)
O, thank You, beloved Friend.

Each time I read the **Big Book** to find prayers for my own meditation, I find new ones, of course. This is how they are for me today. Use these, take others, make your own, but be kind to yourself through prayer and meditation. If it is hard to begin the prayerful attitude (out of which we may have trained ourselves), <u>fake</u> <u>it</u>—act as if your feeling is as deep as anyone else's. Read these or similar words, pretend to let go until something new comes to you. Keep sharing with other people. Every one of them will give you something you need. Good luck.

Nathan P.

0-595-28481-7